Amazon Fargate Quick Start Guide

Learn how to use AWS Fargate to run containers with ease

Deepak Vohra

BIRMINGHAM - MUMBAI

Amazon Fargate Quick Start Guide

Commissioning Editor: Vijin Boricha
Acquisition Editor: Noyonika Das
Content Development Editor: Kirk Dsouza
Technical Editor: Jinesh Topiwala
Copy Editor: Safis Editing
Project Coordinator: Hardik Bhinde
Proofreader: Safis Editing
Indexer: Priyanka Dhadke
Graphics: Jason Monteiro
Production Coordinator: Arvindkumar Gupta

First published: July 2018

Production reference: 1200718

Published by Packt Publishing Ltd.
Livery Place
35 Livery Street
Birmingham
B3 2PB, UK.

ISBN 978-1-78934-501-8

www.packtpub.com

`mapt.io`

Mapt is an online digital library that gives you full access to over 5,000 books and videos, as well as industry leading tools to help you plan your personal development and advance your career. For more information, please visit our website.

Why subscribe?

- Spend less time learning and more time coding with practical eBooks and Videos from over 4,000 industry professionals

- Improve your learning with Skill Plans built especially for you

- Get a free eBook or video every month

- Mapt is fully searchable

- Copy and paste, print, and bookmark content

PacktPub.com

Did you know that Packt offers eBook versions of every book published, with PDF and ePub files available? You can upgrade to the eBook version at `www.PacktPub.com` and as a print book customer, you are entitled to a discount on the eBook copy. Get in touch with us at `service@packtpub.com` for more details.

At `www.PacktPub.com`, you can also read a collection of free technical articles, sign up for a range of free newsletters, and receive exclusive discounts and offers on Packt books and eBooks.

Contributors

About the author

Deepak Vohra is consultant and principle a member of the NuBean software company. He is a **Sun Certified Java Programmer** (**SCJP**) and **Sun Certified Web Component Developer** (**SCWCD**) and has worked in the fields of XML, Java programming, and J2EE for over 10 years. He is the coauthor of the Apress book *Pro XML Development with Java Technology*. Deepak is the author of several Packt Publishing books, including *Processing XML documents* with *Oracle JDeveloper 11g* and *Java EE Development with Eclipse*. Deepak is also a Docker Mentor and has published four other Docker-related books.

About the reviewer

Andrey Zhmaylik is a polyglot systems architect working in Ziftsolutions for Oxford, UK. He has more than 10 years of software development experience with various technology stacks and across different roles in the industry, from software development engineering to leading development teams.

Packt is searching for authors like you

If you're interested in becoming an author for Packt, please visit `authors.packtpub.com` and apply today. We have worked with thousands of developers and tech professionals, just like you, to help them share their insight with the global tech community. You can make a general application, apply for a specific hot topic that we are recruiting an author for, or submit your own idea.

Table of Contents

Preface

At AWS re:Invent 2017, a new launch type for containers called Fargate was announced. This book is about Amazon Fargate, the new launch type for the Amazon **Elastic Container Service (ECS)** for Docker containers.

Docker is the de factostandard containerization framework that has revolutionized packaging and deployment of software. Amazon Fargate has made the ECS platform serverless; no EC2 instances to provision, run, or manage. Amazon Fargate runs ECS services on Docker containers and exposes the service tasks directly to the user. Fargate has much simplified the ECS platform by making it serverless.

Amazon Fargate provides the following benefits:

- It's supported on AWS ECS, with support to be added on AWS EKS
- It's fully integrated with the other AWS services, including IAM, CloudWatch Logs, and EC2 Load Balancing
- Amazon Fargate is serverless and reduces management of ECS clusters; no EC2 instances to provision, create, or manage
- ECS service tasks are directly exposed to user
- An Elastic Network Interface is created for each task
- There's support for the auto scaling of ECS tasks
- An ECS CLI is provided to create ECS clusters and deploy tasks with Docker Compose

Instead of launching ECS clusters on EC2 instances, Amazon Fargate launches clusters on the Fargate platform.

Who this book is for

The primary audience is Docker users and developers. Also, if you occupy any of the following roles, you will find this book useful:

- DevOps architect
- Docker specialist
- DevOps engineer (Docker)

What this book covers

Chapter 1, *Getting Started with Amazon ECS and Amazon Fargate*, is an introductory chapter in which we discuss the benefits of using the Fargate launch type, how compute resources are distributed and configured with Fargate launch type, the ECS objects in Fargate that are the same as for the EC2 launch type, and the new features in Fargate.

Chapter 2, *Networking*, introduces the Fargate launch type as used with an ECS cluster. We will create a cluster, including container, task, and service definitions, using a Hello World Docker image. Subsequently, we will invoke the Hello World application using the IPv4 Public IP of the Elastic Network Interface associated with a task.

Chapter 3, *Using CloudWatch Logs*, discusses configuring an ECS container for logging. We demonstrated CloudWatch Logs using an ECS service for MySQL database. The only supported log driver for the Fargate launch type is the awslogs driver.

Chapter 4, *Using Auto Scaling*, introduces ECS service auto scaling as used with the Fargate launch type. Configuring auto scaling involves setting a range (minimum and maximum) for a number of tasks, within which auto scaling is applied.

Chapter 5, *Using IAM*, discusses configuring an IAM user for ECS. The root user does not require any permissions configuration and has access to the ECS resources, ECS Console, ECS API, and all the required AWS services. If an IAM user is to be used with ECS, the required IAM policies must be added to the IAM user.

Chapter 6, *Using an Application Load Balancer*, discusses configuring an ECS service with the Fargate launch type with an application load balancer to balance the HTTP requests for a Hello World service.

Chapter 7, *Using Amazon ECS CLI* , discusses using the ECS CLI to create a cluster of the Fargate launch type. Then, we will deploy a Docker Compose file on the cluster to run a task for a WordPress Docker image.

To get the most out of this book

You should have prior knowledge of Docker, as the Fargate platform is a launch mode for Amazon ECS, a managed service for Docker containers. You should also have some prior knowledge of AWS and ECS.

If you do not already have one, you will need to create an AWS account at `https://aws.amazon.com/resources/create-account/`.

Download the example code files

You can download the example code files for this book from your account at
`www.packtpub.com`. If you purchased this book elsewhere, you can visit
`www.packtpub.com/support` and register to have the files emailed directly to you.

You can download the code files by following these steps:

1. Log in or register at `www.packtpub.com`.
2. Select the **SUPPORT** tab.
3. Click on **Code Downloads & Errata**.
4. Enter the name of the book in the **Search** box and follow the onscreen instructions.

Once the file is downloaded, please make sure that you unzip or extract the folder using the latest version of:

- WinRAR/7-Zip for Windows
- Zipeg/iZip/UnRarX for Mac
- 7-Zip/PeaZip for Linux

The code bundle for the book is also hosted on GitHub
at `https://github.com/PacktPublishing/Amazon-Fargate-Quick-Start-Guide`. In case
there's an update to the code, it will be updated on the existing GitHub repository.

We also have other code bundles from our rich catalog of books and videos available
at `https://github.com/PacktPublishing/`. Check them out!

Download the color images

We also provide a PDF file that has color images of the screenshots/diagrams used in this
book. You can download it here:
`http://www.packtpub.com/sites/default/files/downloads/AmazonFargateQuickStartGu ide_ColorImages.pdf`.

Conventions used

There are a number of text conventions used throughout this book.

`CodeInText`: Indicates code words in text, database table names, folder names, filenames,
file extensions, pathnames, dummy URLs, user input, and Twitter handles. Here is an
example: "Verify that the version is 3.0 with the `get-host` command."

A block of code is set as follows:

```
{
    "Version": "2012-10-17",
    "Statement": [
        {
            "Sid": "",
            "Effect": "Allow",
            "Principal": {
                "Service": "ecs-tasks.amazonaws.com"
            },
            "Action": "sts:AssumeRole"
        }
    ]
}
```

Any command-line input or output is written as follows:

```
Set-ExecutionPolicy RemoteSigned
```

Bold: Indicates a new term, an important word, or words that you see onscreen. For example, words in menus or dialog boxes appear in the text like this. Here is an example: "The **Edit container** dialog gets displayed."

Warnings or important notes appear like this.

Tips and tricks appear like this.

Get in touch

Feedback from our readers is always welcome.

General feedback: Email feedback@packtpub.com and mention the book title in the subject of your message. If you have questions about any aspect of this book, please email us at questions@packtpub.com.

Errata: Although we have taken every care to ensure the accuracy of our content, mistakes do happen. If you have found a mistake in this book, we would be grateful if you would report this to us. Please visit www.packtpub.com/submit-errata, selecting your book, clicking on the Errata Submission Form link, and entering the details.

Piracy: If you come across any illegal copies of our works in any form on the Internet, we would be grateful if you would provide us with the location address or website name. Please contact us at copyright@packtpub.com with a link to the material.

If you are interested in becoming an author: If there is a topic that you have expertise in and you are interested in either writing or contributing to a book, please visit authors.packtpub.com.

Reviews

Please leave a review. Once you have read and used this book, why not leave a review on the site that you purchased it from? Potential readers can then see and use your unbiased opinion to make purchase decisions, we at Packt can understand what you think about our products, and our authors can see your feedback on their book. Thank you!

For more information about Packt, please visit packtpub.com.

Getting Started with Amazon ECS and Amazon Fargate

1

Docker can be installed on the most commonly used OS platforms. CoreOS has Docker pre-installed, and is designed specifically for running Docker containers. Docker for AWS provides an out-of-the-box Docker swarm mode in which a cluster of nodes, called a swarm, provides a distributed platform for running Docker container applications.

Problem: All the aforementioned Docker platforms are only different types of Docker installations, and require Docker containers to run and be managed on the command line.

Solution: Amazon **ECS (Elastic Container Service)** is a managed service for Docker containers with built-in support for scaling, load balancing, networking, storage, logging, and other Docker container management tasks. Amazon ECS supports two launch types: EC2 and Fargate.

With the EC2 launch type, EC2 instances are started to run Docker containers. The Fargate launch type, which was introduced recently (November 2017), hosts tasks that encapsulate Docker containers. The tasks are directly made accessible to the user via an **Elastic Network Interface (ENI)**. The EC2 instances on which Fargate is provisioned are not exposed to the user and are not directly accessible.

In this chapter, we will learn about the following:

- What Amazon Fargate is
- Benefits of Fargate
- Amazon ECS objects
- Compute resources in Amazon ECS Fargate
- What's new in the Amazon Fargate launch type mode?

What Amazon Fargate is

Amazon Fargate is a new launch type for Amazon ECS and Amazon **EKS** (**Elastic Kubernetes Service**)-managed orchestration services for Docker containers on AWS. With the Fargate launch type, the infrastructure is fully provisioned by Fargate. It is serverless, and no EC2 instances are exposed to the user. Docker containers are defined as container definitions within a task definition. A service implements the task definition to run one or more tasks. Each task is associated with an ENI. If the auto-assignment of the public IP at the task level is enabled, a public IP on which an external client may access a task is automatically assigned to a task. Tasks communicate with each other over a private IP.

Benefits of Fargate

The benefits in ECS are as follows:

- A managed service for containerized applications that does not require much user input to run Docker applications
- Microservices consisting of multiple applications run in isolated containers
- Auto scales tasks based on application load
- Integrates with other AWS services including IAM, CloudWatch Logs, Elastic Load Balancing, CloudFormation templates, EBS Volumes, Batch, ECR, and CloudTrail logs
- A **virtual private cloud** (**VPC**) with no resources shared with other users
- Provides support for running a CodePipeline with ECS as the deployment platform
- Supports the latest Docker version 17.0

Fargate provides the following additional benefits:

- With a Fargate launch type, a user does not create or manage any EC2 instances, as none are exposed on the cluster.
- Tasks are directly exposed to the user via an ENI.
- The underlying infrastructure is provisioned by Fargate. EC2 instances are not to be managed with the Fargate launch type.
- CodePipeline supports Fargate as a deployment platform.

- Microservices based on Container definitions encapsulated in a task definition are explicitly linked, and are not to be linked with any additional options, such as links.
- CloudWatch Logs may be auto configured.

Amazon ECS objects

Amazon ECS objects with Fargate are the same as for the EC2 launch type. An ECS cluster is the outermost encapsulation, and it consists of one or more services. A cluster could be distributed over multiple availability zones. A service is an implementation of a task definition, and runs one or more tasks. A task definition could have one or more task revisions. A task revision is a distinct task definition with a set of tasks and a service associated with it. One Fargate instance is associated with a set of tasks in a service. A task definition consists of zero or more container definitions. Typically, a task definition would be associated with one or more container definitions, and a task definition that does not consist of any container definition would not run any task containers. A diagram of ECS objects is shown as follows:

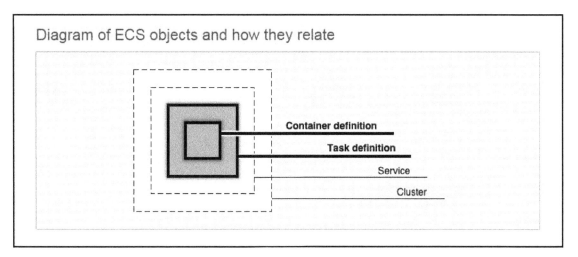

Diagram of ECS objects and how they relate

A **Task definition** is an application template and describes one or more containers. While some attributes or settings are configured at the task level, most of them are configured at the container level. Multiple revisions may be associated with a task definition.

A **Service** implements a task definition, and defines a desired count for tasks to run for a task definition. Optional features such as auto scaling and load balancing are configured in the service.

A **Cluster** in an ECS service is a grouping of one or more container services. A cluster name must be unique within an account. A cluster called default is provisioned by default.

Compute resources in Amazon ECS Fargate

Task size consists of **Task memory (GB)** and **Task CPU (vCPU)**. While optional in the EC2 launch type, task size is required with the Fargate launch type. Docker container level memory and CPU settings may optionally be defined, but are overridden by task definition level settings. Only specific combinations of task memory and task CPU are supported, and the ECS wizard indicates with a message the supported value (or range of values) for a selected value. As an example, the valid CPU range for 1 GB memory is 0.25 vCPU to 0.5 vCPU. The total resources (memory or CPU) configured at the container level must not exceed the task level resource settings. As an example, if a task definition consists of two containers (MySQL and WordPress) with a memory limit of 128 MB for each container, the task level memory must be at least 256 MB. Also, the total of container level memory must not exceed 256 MB. Similarly for the CPU. Two memory limits may be defined at the container level: **Soft limit** and **Hard limit**. The Soft limit corresponds to the `memoryReservation` attribute at the task level, and the Hard limit corresponds to the `memory` attribute at the task level. The sum of container memory reservations (Soft limits) must not exceed the task memory. The Hard limit for each container must not exceed the memory configured at the task level. A minimum of 4 GB must be specified by default for a container.

An example task size is shown in the following screenshot, in which the **Task memory** (`memory` attribute) is set to **0.5 GB** (512 GB), and the **Task CPU** is set to **0.25 vCPU**. At the container level, as configured in the two container definitions, the memory reservation is 128 MB for each container, which makes the total memory reservation of **256 MB** well within the **512 GB** allocated at the task level. The task size is allocated to a task, whether used or not. Similarly, the number of **CPU Units** configured for each container is **10**, which makes the total CPU units 20 for containers within the CPU units, 25 are allocated at the task level. Refer to the following screenshot:

Task size configuration and allocation for containers

What is new in the Amazon Fargate launch type mode?

In addition to and concomitant with the Fargate benefits discussed earlier, Fargate supports the following new features:

- Networking mode, `awsvpc`, is the only supported mode
- Host port mappings are not valid with the Fargate launch type networking mode (`awsvpc`), and host ports on which an application is exposed are the same as the container ports

- `ecsTaskExecutionRole` is added for the Fargate launch type to allow for pulling Docker images and sending logs to CloudWatch Logs
- Only the `awslogs` log configuration and `awslogs` log driver are supported with CloudWatch Logs
- Task placement is not supported, as no ECS instances are provisioned to define placement constraints for
- Only Docker images on Docker Hub and Amazon ECR are supported
- Privileged Windows containers are not supported for the Fargate launch type
- Host devices cannot be exposed to a container
- The `host` and `sourcePath` parameters for volumes are not supported with the Fargate launch type

Summary

In this introductory chapter, we discussed the benefits of using the Fargate launch type, how compute resources are distributed and configured with the Fargate launch type, how the ECS objects with Fargate are the same as for the EC2 launch type, and the new features in Fargate. In the next chapter, we shall discuss networking as used with Fargate.

2
Networking

Amazon ECS is a managed service for containerized applications based on Docker containers. Managed service implies that ECS manages all container orchestration aspects including launching a cluster of virtual machines (EC2 instances), creating and scheduling containers on the virtual machines, and scaling the cluster of VMs.

Problem: Amazon ECS runs Docker containers on virtual machines (EC2 instances). The EC2 launch type incurs an overhead of launching and managing a cluster of virtual machines (EC2 instances). As a primer on ECS, a task definition defines a group of containers (container definitions). A container definition defines a name, Docker image, port mappings, entry point, and command. Resources (CPU and memory) are defined at both the task and container level. A service definition defines a service and consists of a task definition, launch type, load balancers, network configuration, deployment configuration, and deployments. The ECS cluster with the EC2 launch type is as follows:

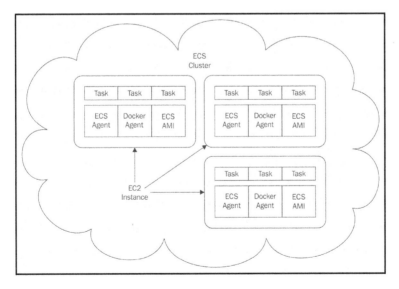

The ECS cluster with the EC2 launch type

Solution: Amazon Fargate has introduced serverless ECS and does not run VMs. The fundamental infrastructure with Fargate is the Fargate platform . A user does not manage the underlying instances, which makes Fargate an **Infrastructure as a Service (IaaS)**. The main benefit of Fargate is that a user does not have to manage any servers. A user does not provision, configure, and scale clusters of VMs. With Fargate, a user does not create or manage any EC2 instances and does not manage cluster capacity and scheduling. A user only has to define the application resource requirements in terms of the CPU and memory of a container and a task, and Fargate manages the scaling as the requirements fluctuate. With the Fargate launch type, ECS is still integrable with all the same AWS services, which include IAM, VPC, and CloudWatch, as it is with the EC2 launch type. The EC2 launch type option is still available. The ECS cluster with the Fargate launch type is illustrated in the following diagram. The only supported networking mode with the Fargate launch type is `awsvpc`, and an elastic network interface for a task is created in a VPC to provide access to the task. An ECS cluster may consist of Fargate-managed tasks in multiple availability zones for high availability:

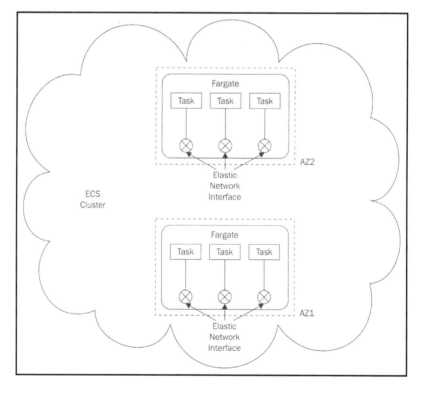

ECS cluster with the Fargate launch type

With the introduction of the Fargate launch type, some of the settings in a task definition, container definition, and service definition are different to the EC2 launch type. The Fargate-related configuration parameters are discussed in subsequent sections.

In this chapter, we will learn about the following:

- Creating an ECS cluster
- Configuring a container definition
- Configuring a task definition
- Configuring a service
- Configuring and creating a cluster
- Running an additional task
- Accessing the service
- Deleting a cluster

The only prerequisite is an AWS account, which may be created at `https://aws.amazon. com/resources/create-account/`.

Creating an ECS cluster and service

Select Amazon ECS and click on **Get Started** to start creating an ECS cluster and service. First, a container definition and a task definition are configured, and subsequently the service and cluster are configured to create the ECS objects cluster, service, task definition, and container definition. We shall discuss configuring each of the these in the following sub-sections.

Configuring a Container definition

The Amazon ECS wizard gets started. A diagram of ECS objects gets displayed, as shown in `Chapter 1`, *Getting Started with Amazon ECS and Amazon Fargate.* By default, the Fargate launch type is used. First, the container definition is to be defined, followed by the task definition.

A Task definition consists of one or more container definitions. Most of the attributes are defined in the container definition, but a few are defined at the task level. To start with, select a container definition template, including the image, from one of those listed, which include **sample-app** and **nginx**, or create a custom container definition.

- Click on **Configure** for the **custom** container definition, as shown in the following screenshot, to create a new custom container definition:

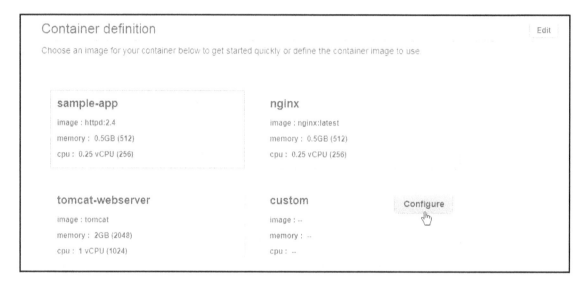

- The **Edit container** dialog gets displayed. The standard configuration for a container includes the fields discussed in the following table:

Field	Description
Container name	The name of the Docker container to be created.
Image	The Docker image.
Port mappings	Container port mappings. Host port mappings are not supported with Fargate and default to the same value as the container port mappings.

- Specify a **Container name** (hello-world). Click on the **i** icon to display a callout for the container name. The container name must be up to 255 characters (uppercase and lowercase, numbers, hyphens, and underscores).
- Next, specify a Docker **Image** (tutum/hello-world). The image name must be up to 255 characters (uppercase and lowercase, numbers, hyphens, underscores, colons, periods, /, and number signs). The Fargate launch type only supports images in the Amazon ECR or public repositories in Docker Hub.
- Next, specify the Memory Limits in MiB. Two memory limits may be specified: **Soft limit** and **Hard limit**. Either or both may be specified. The effect of specifying one or both is discussed in this table:

Memory types configured	Description
Soft limit only	ECS reserves the specified amount of memory (memoryReservation) for the container. The container may request more memory in excess of the soft limit up to all of the memory that is available on the container instance.
Hard limit only	The memory requested by the container cannot exceed the hard limit.
Both Soft limit and Hard limit	ECS reserves a specified amount of memory (memoryReservation) for the container. The container may request more memory in excess of the soft limit up to the hard limit if specified, or all of the memory that is available on the container instance, whichever it reaches first. If both are specified, the Hard limit must be greater or the same as the Soft limit.

- The dropdown for the **Memory Limits** lists both the **Hard Limit** and the **Soft limit**. The **Soft limit** default value, is **128 MiB**. To add a hard limit on memory in addition to a soft limit, click on the **Add Hard Limit** link. A Hard limit gets added. **Memory Limits** are shown as follows. The **Soft limit** (128 MiB) is less than the **Hard limit** (256 MiB):

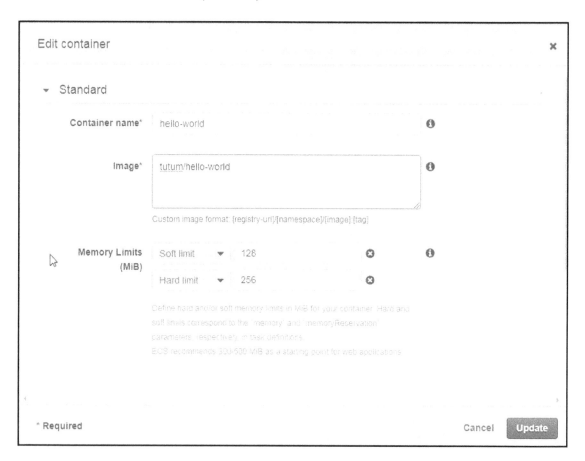

- Next, specify the **Port mappings**. With the Fargate launch type, exposed ports must be specified as container ports. Container port 80 is specified as follows. The host port is the same as the **Container port** by default, and cannot be set to a different value with the awsvpc network mode that the Fargate launch type uses:

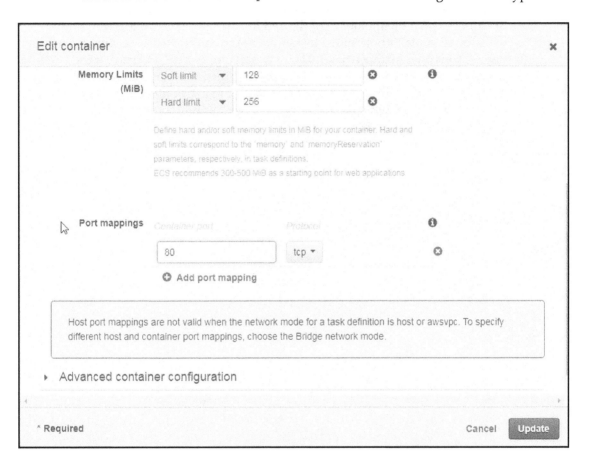

- Optionally, specify **Advanced container configuration**, which consists of configuration for Environment, Network settings, Storage & Logging, Resource Limits, and Docker Labels. While the memory and CPU configuration is required at the task definition level, it is optional at the container level. The only requirement is that the total amount of memory for all containers within a task must not exceed the memory configured for the task, and the total amount of CPU for all containers within a task must not exceed the CPU configured for the task. A container instance has 1,024 CPU units for every CPU core. If the **Essential** checkbox for a container is checked, the failure of the container returns in the entire task failing. At least one container in a task must be set as the essential container, which implies that if a task has only one container, it must be essential, as shown here:

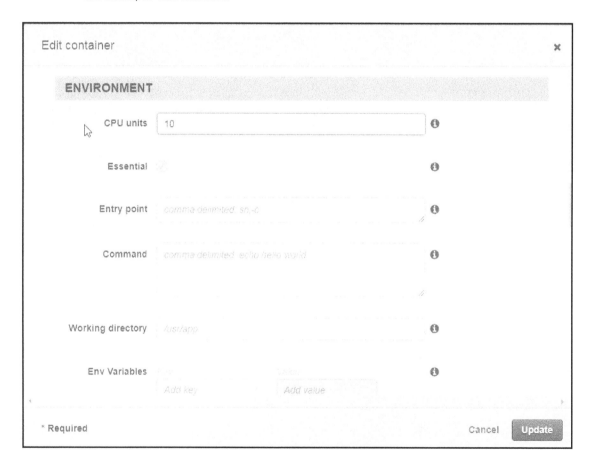

- The only network mode supported by the Fargate launch type is `awsvpc`. The only supported log configuration and log driver for the Fargate launch type is awslogs. Click on **Update** after configuring the custom container, shown as follows:

- A **Container definition** for the **hello-world** custom container gets added as follows:

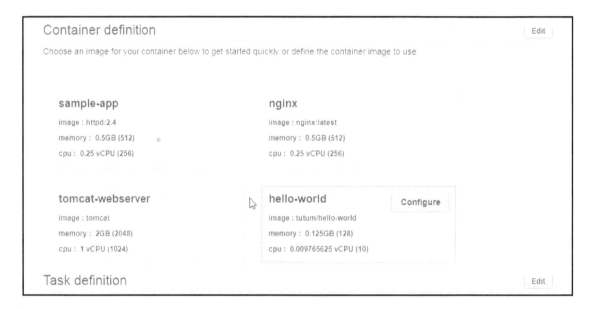

Configuring a Task definition

The task definition has a default name, which may be modified. The **Network mode** is **awsvpc** and cannot be modified. The **Task execution role** is **Create new**. The **Task execution role** is the IAM role assumed by the ECS to access the resources needed by a task and includes permissions to pull private Docker images and publish logs for a task. **Compatibilities** (launch type) is **FARGATE**. **Task memory** is **0.5 GB** by default, and **Task CPU** is **0.25 vCPU** by default. The default **Task definition** is shown as follows:

- Click on **Edit** to modify any of the task settings if required:

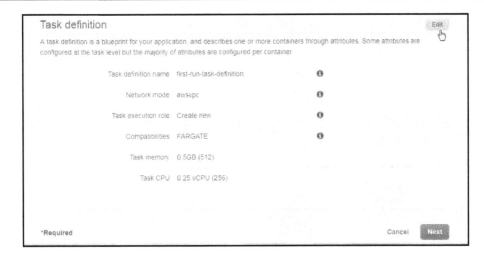

- The **Configure task definition** window gets displayed, as shown in the following screenshot. Specify **Task definition name** (hello-world-task-definition) and select a **Task execution role** (or keep the default role):

- The **Task size** is the total CPU and memory used by the task. The **Task memory** and **Task CPU** values constitute a bucket and only supported memory values for a selected CPU may be specified. The range of memory values supported for a given CPU may be obtained from the section **Task Size** table at `https://docs.aws.amazon.com/AmazonECS/latest/developerguide/task_definition_parameters.html`. If the Task memory is not within the supported range for the selected Task CPU, an error gets generated. Set **Task memory** to **1 GB** and **Task CPU** to **0.5 vCPU**. Click on **Save** to save the task configuration as follows:

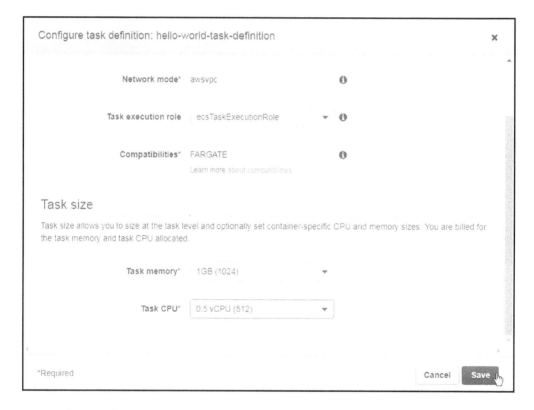

- After configuring the container definition and task definition, the task definition summary is shown in the following screenshot. Click on **Next** to complete the container and task definitions:

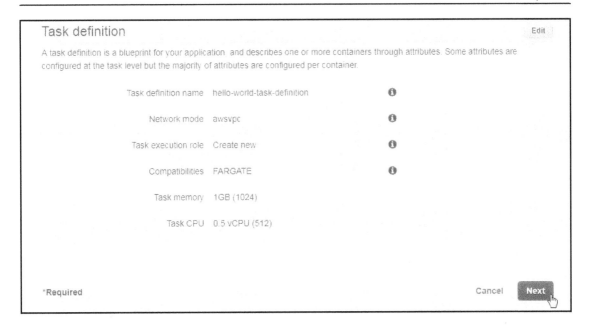

Configuring a service

Next, configure the service. The default settings for the service create one task as indicated by the **Number of desired tasks**. Additional tasks may be added after a service has been created, as discussed in a later section. A new security group is created automatically as indicated by the **Security group** field/label, and the option to create a custom security group is not provided. A security group is created to allow all public traffic to a service on the container port(s) configured. Network access and security groups may be further configured outside the wizard. The **Load balancer type** is **None** by default, with the option to select **Application Load Balancer**. Using an Application Load Balancer is discussed in Chapter 6, *Using an Application Load Balancer*.

If an application load balancer is to be added, it must be created before creating the ECS cluster.

- Click on **Next** to complete the service configuration:

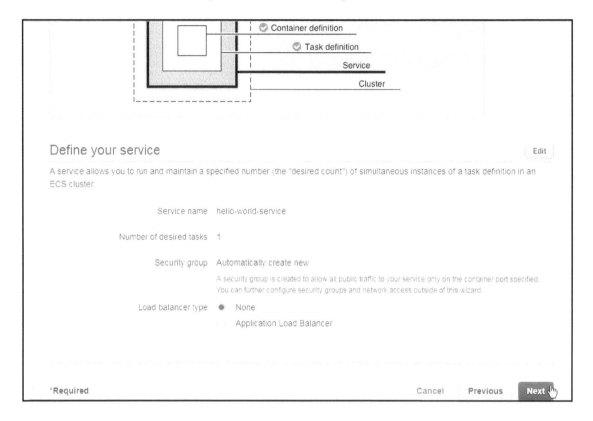

Define your service

A service allows you to run and maintain a specified number (the "desired count") of simultaneous instances of a task definition in an ECS cluster.

Service name	hello-world-service
Number of desired tasks	1
Security group	Automatically create new
	A security group is created to allow all public traffic to your service only on the container port specified. You can further configure security groups and network access outside of this wizard.
Load balancer type	● None
	○ Application Load Balancer

Configuring and creating a cluster

Next, configure the cluster:

- Specify a **Cluster name** (hello-world) with the default cluster name being **default**.

- The **VPC ID** setting specifies the ID of the VPC to be used by the container. By default, a new VPC is created automatically. The **Subnets** setting specifies the ID of the subnet to be used by the container. A subnet is a range of IP addresses in a VPC. By default, new subnets are created automatically. Click on **Next** to complete the cluster configuration:

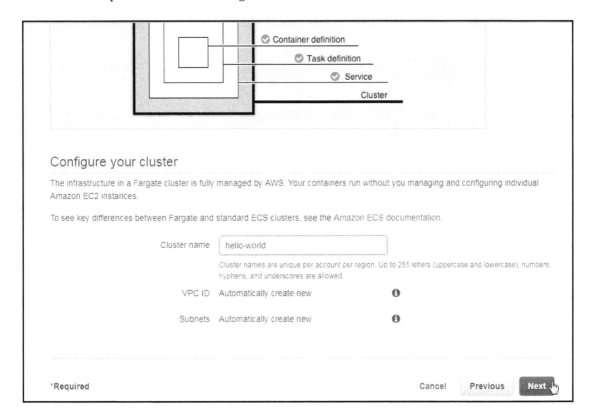

- Review the ECS to be created. To modify **Task definition**, **Service**, or **Cluster**, click on the associated **Edit**. To create the Amazon ECS with the launch type as Fargate, click on **Create**:

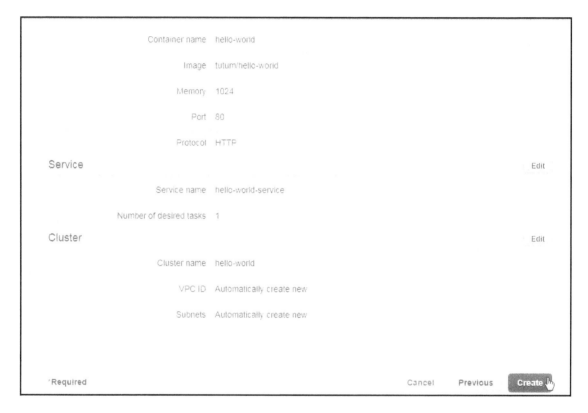

- The Amazon Elastic Service with the Fargate launch type begins to get created. The **Launch Status** displayed indicates the resource status as complete or pending. The complete status is for resources that have been created and the pending status is for resources that are in the process of being created. When all of the service resources have been created, click on **View service**:

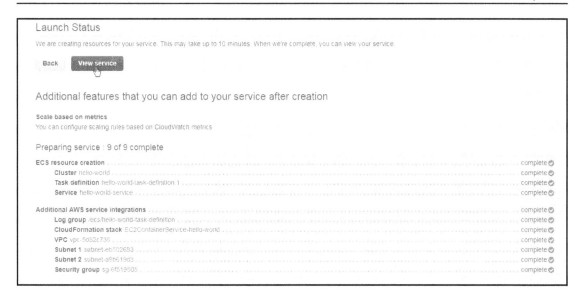

The service summary gets displayed. In addition to the service name, the service summary includes **Cluster**, **Status**, **Task definition**, **Launch type**, **Platform version**, **Service role**, **Desired count**, **Pending count**, and **Running count**. The **Details** tab is selected by default. As we did not add load balancing, the **Load Balancing** header indicates **No load balancers**. The **Network Access** header lists the **Auto-Assign Public IP** as **Enabled**, and these are all shown as follows:

To list the tasks in the service, select the **Tasks** tab. One task is listed, as we configured only one task. The **Task status** is **Running** or **Stopped**. The tasks table columns are **Task** (name), **Task definition**, **Last status**, **Desired status**, **Group**, **Launch type**, and **Platform version**:

The **Events** tab lists the events. Each event is associated with an **Event Id**, **Event Time**, and **Message**:

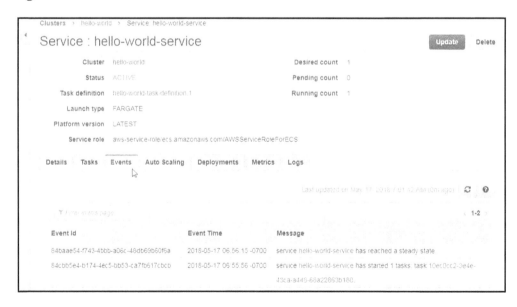

The **Deployment**s tab lists the **Task Placement Strategy** and **Constraint**. Task placement constraints are not supported with the Fargate launch type:

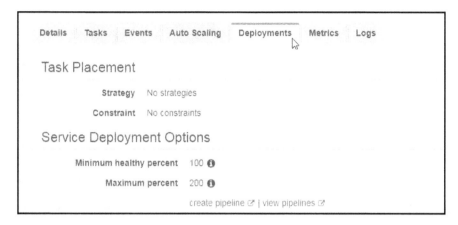

To display the metrics, which include **CPUUtilization** and **MemoryUtilization**, select the **Metrics** tab. **Minimum**, **Maximum**, and **Average** values are color coded, as indicated in the screenshot legend:

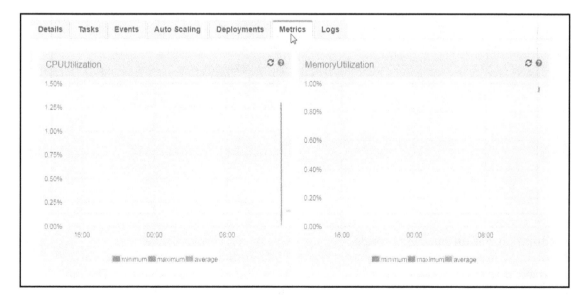

To display the logs, select the **Logs** tab:

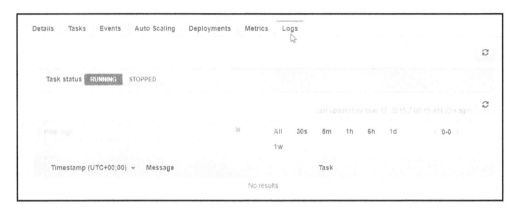

The **Clusters** list a **hello-world** cluster of the Fargate launch type and no EC2 clusters are shown:

A **CloudFormation** stack gets created for the ECS cluster, shown in the following **CloudFormation** dashboard. The AWS **CloudFormation** dashboard can be accessed at `https://us-east-2.console.aws.amazon.com/cloudformation`. The table lists the stacks with columns for **Stack Name**, **Created Time**, **Status**, and **Description**. Tabs for **Overview**, **Outputs**, **Resources**, **Events**, **Template**, **Parameters**, **Tags**, **Stack Policy**, and **Change Sets** are provided. The **Events** tab indicates the **CREATE_COMPLETE** status for resources that have been created:

Running additional tasks

By default, one task is created. In this section, we shall discuss the procedure to add an additional task. The **Tasks** tab in the cluster displays the tasks associated with a cluster:

Tasks associated with a service are listed on the service page. To display a task definition's details, click on the link for the task definition in the Service page or the cluster page. A task definition is shown in the following screenshot:

- To run a new task, select **Actions | Run Task**. A new task gets created with **Run Task:**

- Two options are provided for the launch type to run a new task: **Fargate** and **EC2**. Select the **Fargate** launch type, as shown in the following screenshot.
- The **Task Definition name** is pre-specified. The **Platform version** is LATEST by default.
- The **Cluster** is also selected and, if more than one cluster is available, the cluster may be selected from a drop-down list.
- Specify the **Number of tasks** to create.
- Optionally, specify a **Task Group**. A task group is a set of related tasks, and all tasks in the same task group are considered as a set when performing spread placement. Required fields are marked with an asterisk (*):

- Select a **Cluster VPC** from the dropdown, as shown in the following screenshot.
- In the **Subnets** dropdown, select the subnets. Choose the subnets in the selected VPC that the task scheduler should consider for placement. Only private subnets are currently supported.

- Select **Auto-assign Public IP** as ENABLED. A security group is created by default with port 80 open to the internet:

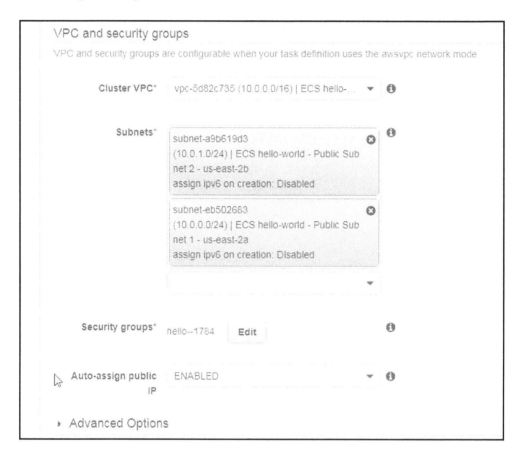

- Advanced options include **Task overrides** and **Container overrides**, as shown in the following screenshot. We have not set any advanced options:

- Click on **Run Task** to run a new task, as shown in the following screenshot:

A task gets created. The message **Created tasks successfully** gets displayed. The message includes **tasks**, even though one new task has been created, because the message is a standard message for creating one or more new tasks. A new task gets listed in the **Tasks** tab, as shown in the following screenshot. The **Last status** column indicates that the task status is **RUNNING**. Initially, the **Last status** is **PROVISIONING**:

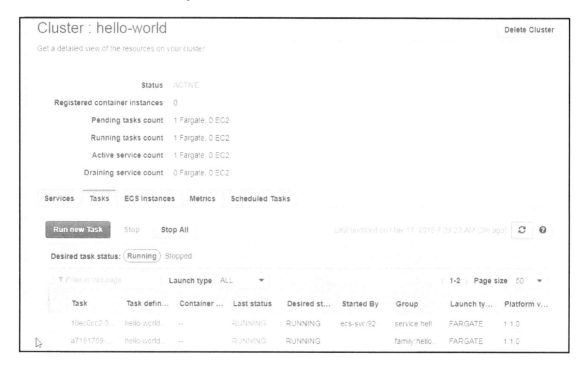

The **hello-world** cluster lists two **Running tasks**, as shown in the following screenshot. The number of **Pending tasks** is listed as **0**:

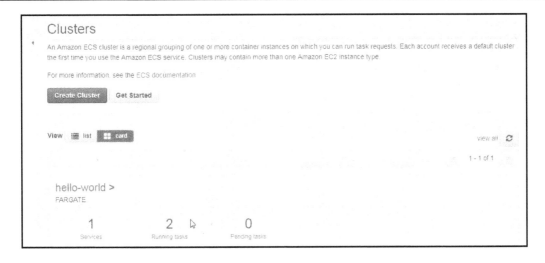

Accessing the service

To be able to access a service, the **Network Access** should be configured with **Auto-assign public IP** as **ENABLED**, as shown in the following screenshot:

To provide network access, an ENI gets created for each task. The ENI is associated with a public IP that may be used to access an application running in a task container:

- Click on the link for a task in **Service** | **Tasks**, as shown in the following screenshot:

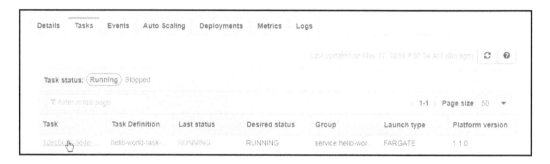

- On the task detail page, click on the link for the **ENI Id**, as shown in the following screenshot:

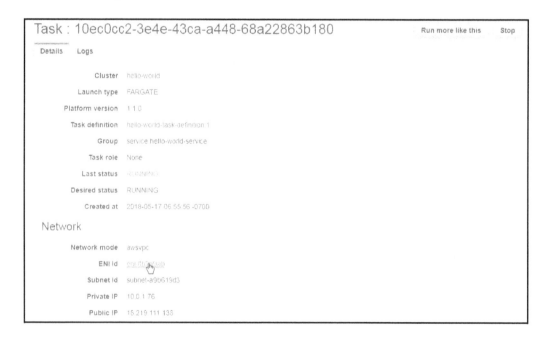

- Copy the **IPv4 Public IP** from the ENI console, **18.219.111.138** in the following screenshot, which would be different for different users:

- Specify the **IPv4 Public IP** in a browser to invoke the **Hello World** application, as shown in the following screenshot:

Deleting a cluster

To delete a cluster, the cluster must not be running any tasks:

- Select all running tasks and click on **Stop**, as shown in the following screenshot. Alternatively, select **Stop All**, without selecting any tasks:

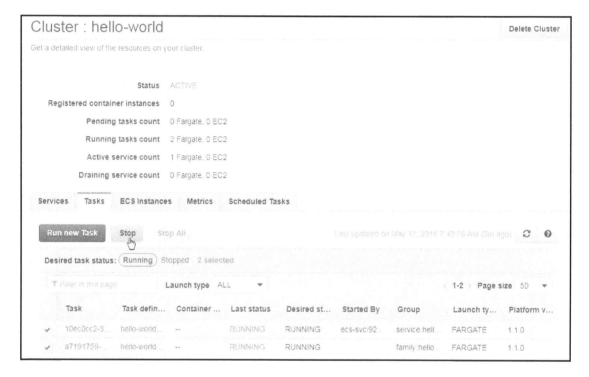

- In the **Stop tasks** confirmation dialog, click on **Stop**. The tasks get stopped, as indicated by the message **Stopped tasks successfully**.

- Click on **Delete Cluster** to delete the cluster:

- In the **Delete Cluster** confirmation dialog, click on **Delete**. The hello-world cluster gets deleted. If the **CoudFormation** stack associated with the cluster times out before the cluster gets deleted, an error message gets displayed, as shown in the following screenshot, and the cluster does not get deleted. If the **CloudFormation** stack does not get deleted automatically when the ECS cluster is chosen to be deleted, click on the **View CloudFormation Stack** link in the error message:

- In the **CloudFormation** | **Stacks** dashboard, select **CloudFormation**, and click on **Actions** | **Delete Stack**, as shown in the following screenshot. **Delete Stack** may need to be initiated after the stack Status becomes **DELETE FAILED**:

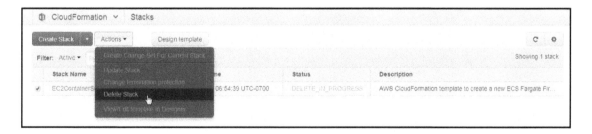

- In the **Delete Stack** confirmation dialog, select all the resources that are to be deleted, along with the **CloudFormation** stack and click on **Yes, Delete**. **CloudFormation** gets deleted. After the **CloudFormation** stack has been deleted, delete the ECS cluster and the ECS cluster should also get deleted.

Summary

In this chapter, we introduced the Fargate launch type as used with an ECS cluster. We created a cluster, including container, task, and service definitions, using a Hello World Docker image. Subsequently, we invoked the Hello World application using the IPv4 public IP of the Elastic Network Interface associated with a task. Some of the container definition and task definition parameters are different for the Fargate launch type in comparison to the EC2 launch type, which is still available as an alternative with ECS. In the next chapter, we shall discuss integrating the CloudWatch Logs service with Fargate.

3
Using CloudWatch Logs

Docker containers generate logs, and Docker supports the `docker logs` and `docker service logs` commands to list logs. Docker also supports logging drivers, which are logging mechanisms to get logs generated by running containers and services.

Problem: Without a managed service, such as Amazon ECS, a logging driver must be configured if a logging mechanism is to be added.

Solution: With the Fargate launch type, logging is greatly simplified and the only supported logging driver is `awslogs`. The `awslogs` logging driver streams logs generated by ECS tasks to CloudWatch Logs. Using `aws-logs-prefix`, a label may be associated with the `awslogs` driver to differentiate between the log streams generated by the different tasks containers.

In this chapter, we will learn about the following:

- Overview of CloudWatch Logs and aws log driver
- Creating an ECS service for a MySQL database
- Configuring a Container definition
- Configuring logging
- Configuring a Task definition
- Configuring a service
- Configuring a cluster
- Creating an ECS service
- Exploring Task Logs
- Exploring CloudWatch Logs
- Exploring CloudWatch metrics

The only prerequisite is an AWS account.

Overview of CloudWatch Logs and aws log driver

Amazon CloudWatch is an AWS service for monitoring logs from AWS resources, including Amazon ECS, EC2, EBS volumes, Elastic Load Balancers, and RDS. Metrics for CPU utilization, memory utilization, latency, and request counts are streamed in near-real time from these resources to CloudWatch. Some CloudWatch terms and concepts are discussed in the following table:

CloudWatch concept	Description
Log event	A `log event`, which includes a log message and a timestamp, is a record of some event/activity on a resource or application.
Log stream	A `log stream` is a continuous sequence of log events from the same resource or application.
Log group	A `log group` is a group of log streams that share the same retention, monitoring, and access control settings. Each log stream is associated with a single log group, and the log streams in a log group do not have to originate from the same resource or application. More often, the log streams originate from different resources or applications, and the log group aggregates similar monitoring data.
Metric filter	Metric filters filter metric observations from events to generate data points for a CloudWatch metric.
Retention settings	Retention settings indicate the duration for which the log events are to be kept.

The `awslogs` log driver is the only log driver supported with the Fargate launch type. The `awslogs` log driver supports the options discussed in the following table. The `awslogs` log driver supports other options in addition to those discussed in the table, but ECS only supports these options:

Option	Description	Required
`awslogs-region`	Specifies the Amazon region to which CloudWatch logs are sent.	Yes
`awslogs-group`	Specifies the log group to which the log streams are to send their logs.	Yes
`awslogs-stream-prefix`	Specifies a prefix that is to be associated with a log stream. Log streams generated with the Fargate launch type have the following format: `prefix-name/container-name/ecs-task-Id`.	Yes, for Fargate launch type

Creating an ECS service for MySQL database

In this section, we shall create an ECS definition for a MySQL database to demonstrate logging. Any Docker image could be used; the MySQL database image was chosen because several log events are generated when MySQL database is inited, installed, and configured. Another Docker image, such as `tutum/hello-world`, does not generate very many log events.

1. Open URL in a browser and click on **Get started with Amazon ECS**. The ECS console starts up.
2. Click on **Get started** to start the wizard to create new container and task definitions, and a new service. By default, the ECS wizard is based on the Fargate launch type. The diagram of ECS objects is displayed.

The ECS objects are discussed in Chapter 1, *Getting Started with Amazon ECS and Amazon Fargate*.

Configuring a Container definition

In this section, we shall discuss creating a container definition for a MySQL database:

1. Click on **Configure** for the **Custom** Container definition, as shown in the following screenshot. Some other container definitions are available as examples:

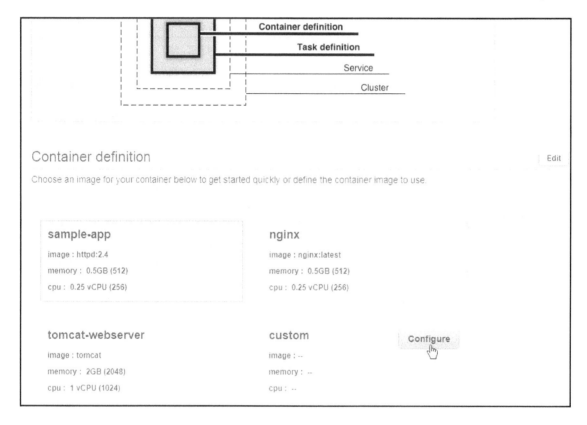

2. In the **Edit container** dialog, specify a **Container name** (mysql) and specify **Image** as mysql, as shown in the following screenshot.

3. Specify a **Soft limit** (512) and a **Hard limit** (1024) for memory. The hard limit for memory must not be less than the soft limit:

4. Specify the **Container port** as `3306` in **Port Mappings**, with the **Protocol** as **tcp**, as shown in the following screenshot. With the Fargate launch type, only container port mappings may be configured. Host port mappings are not valid, and are set to the same value as the container port mappings:

5. In the **Advanced container configuration | ENVIRONMENT** section, specify the mandatory environment variable for the **mysql** Docker image. The mandatory environment variable is `MYSQL_ROOT_PASSWORD` and sets the password for the `root` user, as shown in the following screenshot. Optionally, specify other environment variables such as `MYSQL_DATABASE` for the database to create.

6. The **Essential** checkbox indicates whether a container is essential to the running of a task. If the **Essential** checkbox is selected, the container is essential, and if the container fails, the task fails too. At least one container in a task definition must be set as **Essential**. As the **mysql** container is the only container, it must be set to **Essential**:

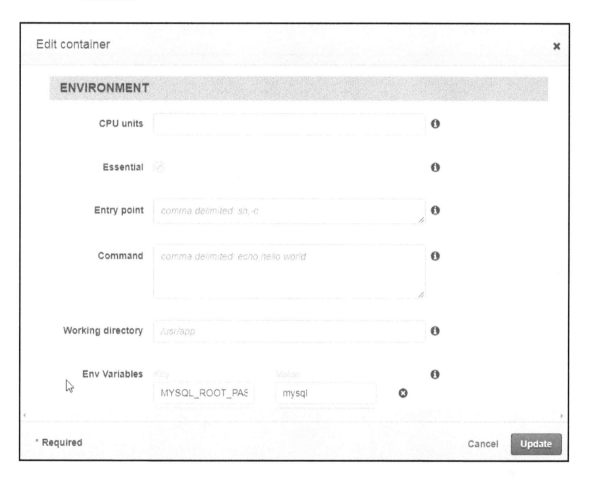

Configuring logging

Scroll to the **STORAGE AND LOGGING** section in the **Edit container** dialog, as shown in the following screenshot:

1. To configure logging automatically, click the **Auto-configure CloudWatch Logs** checkbox. The Fargate launch type only supports the `awslogs` log driver:

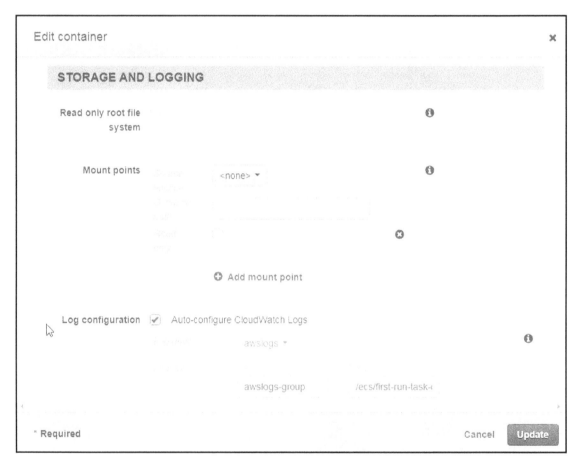

2. All the log options discussed in the earlier table are mandatory for the Fargate launch type, and the default value for each gets set. The `awslogs-group` option is set to a value of `/ecs/<task definition name>`. If the task definition name is modified after configuring the logging, the `awslogs-group` also gets updated. Click on **Update** to complete the container configuration:

The `logConfiguration` parameters added for the logging configuration are as follows:

```
{
        "containerDefinitions": [{
                ...
                "logConfiguration": {
                        "logDriver": "awslogs",
                        "options": {
                                "awslogs-group":
"/ecs/mysql-task-definition",
                                "awslogs-region": "us-
east-1",
                                "awslogs-stream-prefix":
"ecs"
                        }
                }
```

```
                          . . .
            }]
    }
```

A container definition, **mysql**, for the MySQL database gets created as shown in next illustration.

Configuring a Task definition

The default **Task definition** settings are listed. Some of the **Task definition** settings are modifiable, while others are not. **Network mode** is not modifiable, and must be **awsvpc**. **Compatibilities** is also not modifiable, and must be set to **FARGATE**. Modifying the task definition is optional:

1. To modify a task definition, click on **Task definition | Edit**, as shown in the following screenshot:

2. In the **Configure task definition** dialog, set the **Task definition name** (`mysql-task-definition`) as shown in the following screenshot.
3. **Network mode** is not modifiable for the Fargate launch type and must be **awsvpc**.
4. Select **Task execution role** as **ecsTaskExecutionRole**. The **ecsTaskExecutionRole** grants permissions to make calls to CloudWatch to send container logs.
5. **Compatibilities** is preset to **FARGATE,** and is not modifiable either.
6. Set the **Task size**, which allocates the selected task memory and CPU to the task. Only specific combinations of **Task memory** and **Task CPU** may be selected.
7. Click on **Save** to complete the task definition configuration:

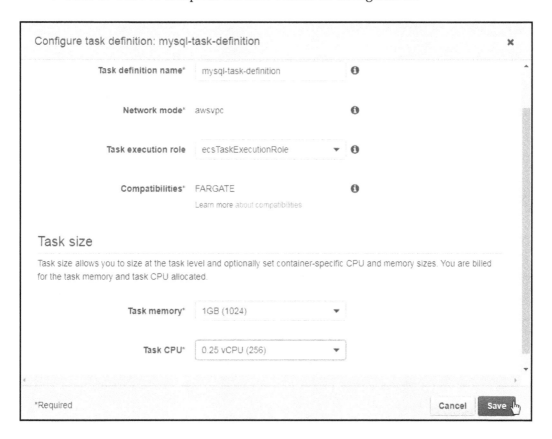

8. The task configuration gets saved. `awslogs-group` gets updated to `/ecs/mysql-task-definition`. Click on **Next** in the Get Started wizard, as shown in the following screenshot:

Configuring a service

Having configured the Container definition and task definition, it's time to configure the service next. The **Service name** (mysql-service), **Number of desired tasks** (**1** by default), **Security group** (**Automatically create new**), and **Load balancer type** (**None**) may be modified if required with **Edit**. We shall use the default settings for the service to demonstrate logging with Fargate. Click on **Next,** as shown in the following screenshot:

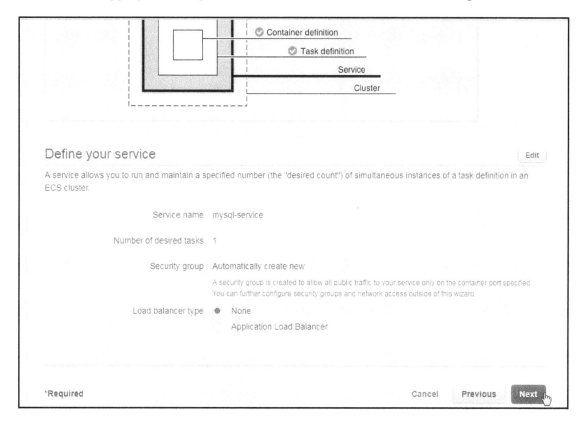

Configuring a cluster

Next, configure the cluster. The default cluster is specified in **Cluster name** by default:

- Specify a different Cluster name (`mysql`).
- The default settings for **VPC ID** and **Subnets** are to create new. Click on **Next**:

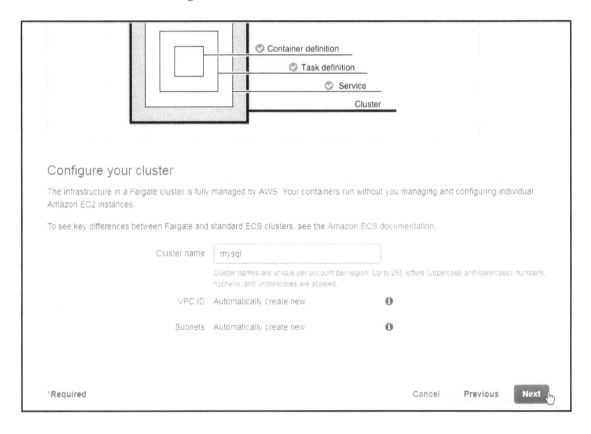

Creating an ECS service

Review the settings for the **Container definition**, **Task definition**, and **Service**. The **Edit** button is provided to edit any of these ECS objects:

1. To create the ECS with the Fargate launch type, click on **Create** in **Review**, as shown in the following screenshot:

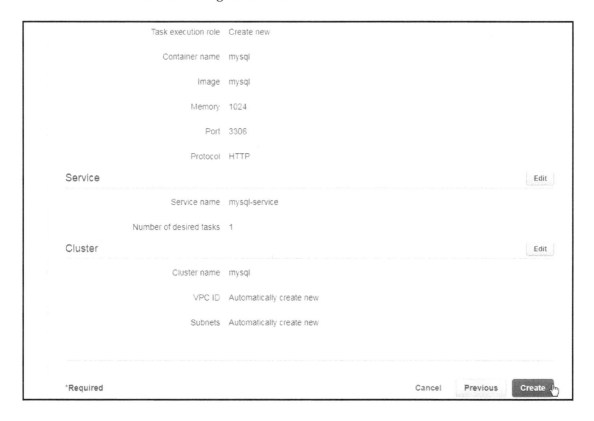

2. The ECS resources start to get created, as shown in **Launch Status** in the following screenshot. Some of the resources are shown as **pending**, while others are shown as **complete**. When all the ECS resources have been created, as indicated by the **complete** status, click on **View service**:

An ECS `mysql-service` gets created in the `mysql` cluster, as listed in the **Services** tab of the **mysql**, cluster as shown in the following screenshot:

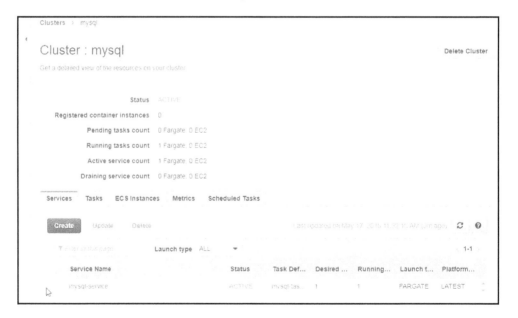

The **Task** tab lists the tasks in the service, as shown in the following screenshot. Click on the task link to list the details of the task:

The task details get displayed, including the **ENI Id** link shown in the following screenshot, in order to obtain details about the ENI. The **Public IP** and **Private IP** for the task definition are also listed:

Click on **Task Definitions** in the margin navigation to list the task definition, including revision, in **Task Definition Name: Revision** format, as shown in the following screenshot. Other task definitions may also be listed. The task definition **Status** is listed as **Active**, which indicates the task definition is active and may be used in a service to run tasks:

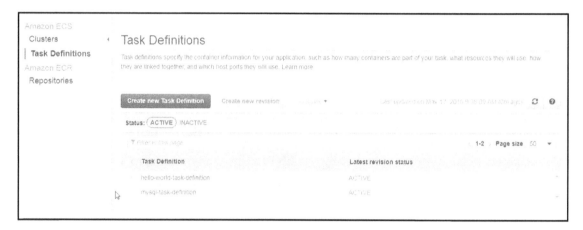

Click on the task definition link to list the task definition's revisions, as shown in the following screenshot:

Click on the task definition revision link to display the **Builder** and **JSON** format tabs, as shown in the following screenshot. To create a new revision of the task definition, click on **Create new revision**. We have not used a new revision, but a new revision creates a new set of tasks, based on a revised task definition:

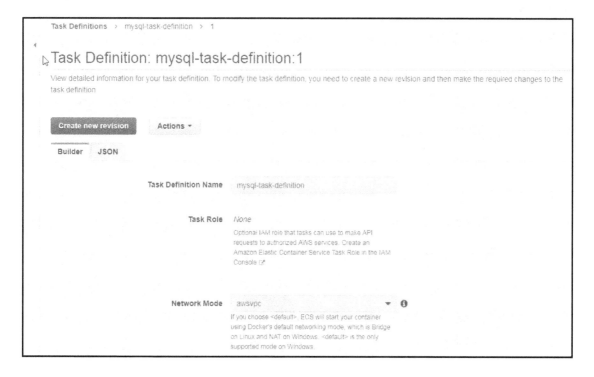

The **mysql** container is listed in the **Container Definitions** section. The **Container Definitions** table lists the **Container Name**, Docker **Image**, **CPU Units**, **Hard/Soft memory limits**, and whether the container is **Essential**. Click on the **mysql** container to display its details, including **Log Configuration**, as shown in the following screenshot. The detailed configuration includes **Port Mappings** and **Environment Variables**:

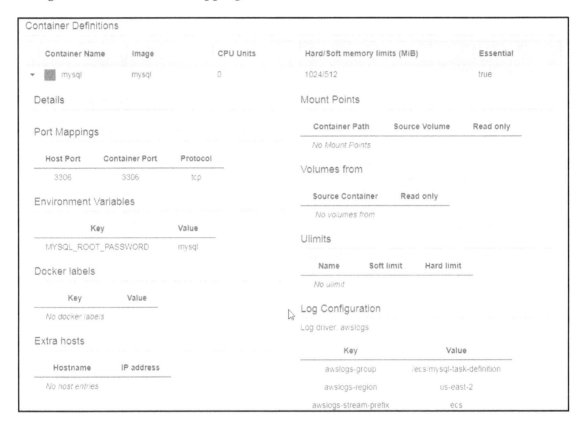

The **mysql** cluster is listed in clusters, as shown in the following screenshot. The number of **Services** and the number of **Running tasks** and **Pending tasks** are also listed. Only the **FARGATE** launch type lists services and tasks, and not the EC2 launch type:

Exploring Task logs

Task log events are generally used for debugging a task or a service, and to find out whether a task started without any errors. The log events generated by a task are displayed by selecting the **Logs** tab in the task details, shown in the following screenshot. Each log entry includes a **Timestamp** and a log **Message**. An example of debugging a task is indicated by a **MySQL init process failed** message:

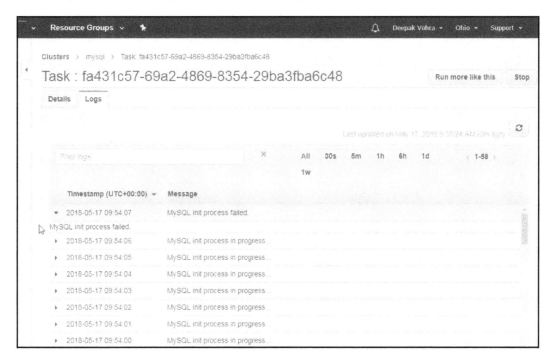

A task could fail for several reasons, and some of the common reasons are:

- Task is out of memory
- Mandatory environment variables have not been set
- Insufficient CPU allocated to the container or task

An example log entry in which a MySQL database is indicated to be running and accepting connections is **mysqld: ready for connections**, as shown in the following screenshot:

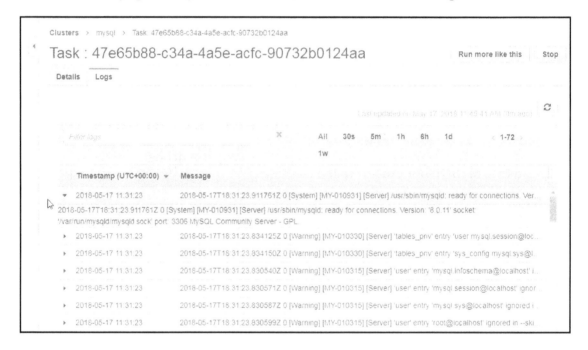

Exploring CloudWatch Logs

In this section, we shall find details about the CloudWatch logs generated and display the log streams generated:

1. Click on **Logs** in the CloudWatch Console, as shown in the following screenshot:

2. In **Filter**, specify `/ecs/mysql` or just `/ecs`, which is the value of the `awslogs-stream-prefix` option for the `awslogs` log driver, as configured in the container definition in the *Configuring logging* section. The log group `/ecs/mysql-task-definition` is displayed, as shown in the following screenshot:

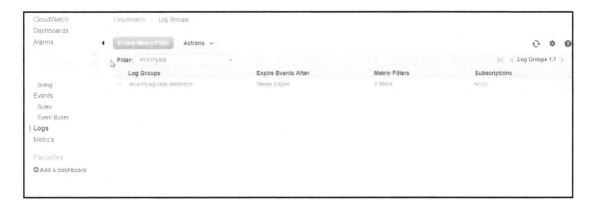

3. Click on the log group to display the log streams, as shown in the following screenshot:

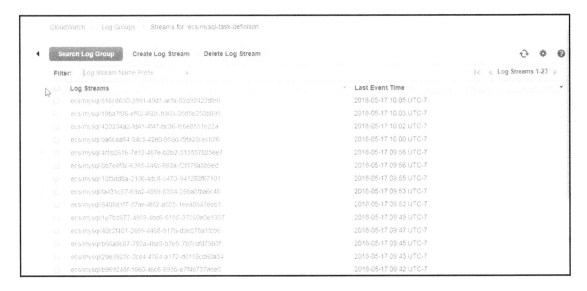

The log events in the log stream get displayed. Each log event is associated with a timestamp and a log message. An example log message is **Initializing database**, as shown in the following screenshot. Some of the messages have **[Warning]** associated with them:

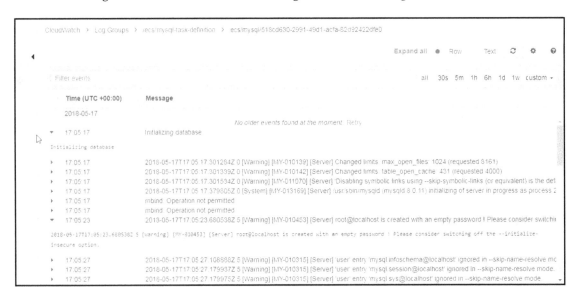

A CloudWatch log message indicating the MySQL database is running and accepting connections is the message **mysqld: ready for connections**, as shown in the following screenshot:

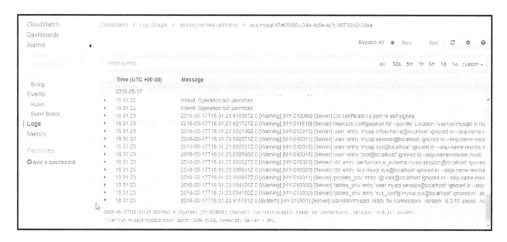

Exploring CloudWatch metrics

In this section, we shall display the metrics:

1. Click on **Metrics** in the navigation, as shown in the following screenshot. Filter metrics for the **mysql** service with **All | ECS ClusterName | ServiceNameSelect** to display all metrics, which include **MemoryUtilization** and **CPUUtilization** metrics:

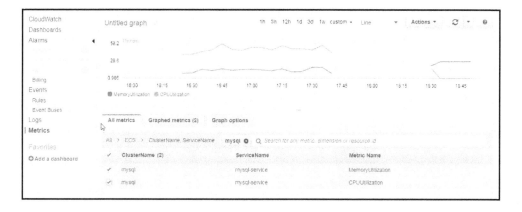

2. Not all metrics may be graphed, although the **MemoryUtilization** and **CPUUtilization** metrics generated by a task are graphed. Select the **Graphed metrics** tab to display only the graphed metrics:

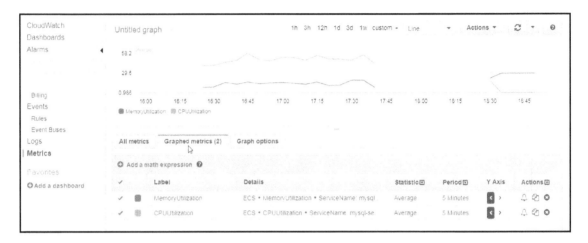

Summary

In this chapter, we discussed configuring an ECS container for logging. We demonstrated CloudWatch Logs using an ECS service for a MySQL database. The only supported log driver for the Fargate launch type is the awslogs driver. Three log driver options must be configured with the Fargate launch type: `awslogs-region`, `awslogs-stream-prefix`, and `awslogs-group`. In the next chapter, we shall discuss auto scaling with Fargate.

4
Using Auto Scaling

Amazon ECS provides built-in internal load balancing to distribute client traffic between the tasks in an ECS service. If all the client load were to be sent to a single task in a three-task service, the internal load balancer would direct some of the client traffic to the other tasks to distribute the client load evenly.

Problem: The number of tasks in a service as configured initially is fixed. If the client load is expected to be fixed, the fixed number of tasks in an ECS service should suffice. But if client load fluctuates, the ECS service tasks do not scale automatically. If the client load were to increase, the preconfigured number of tasks may not be able to serve the client traffic.

Solution: Amazon ECS supports auto scaling using an auto scaling policy that consists of a CloudWatch alarm based on one of the ECS service metrics: `CPUUtilization` or `MemoryUtilization`. An alarm threshold must be set before any scaling action is performed; for instance, `MemoryUtilization` must not exceed a specific value for a specified number of consecutive periods, with each period being one minute, five minutes, 15 minutes, or 1 hour. If an alarm threshold is exceeded, a scaling action could be performed, such as adding, setting to, or removing a specified number or percentage of tasks. The measure of client load is `CPUUtilization` or `MemoryUtilization`.

The number of tasks scale with the load, as illustrated in the following diagram:

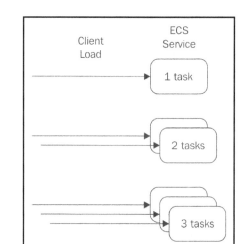

In this chapter, we shall demonstrate configuring and using auto scaling and we will learn about the following:

1. Creating an ECS service for a Hello world application
2. Types of auto scaling
3. Configuring an auto scaling policy
4. Demonstrating the use of auto scaling
5. Exploring CloudWatch metrics and logs
6. Updating a service to modify the number of tasks

Creating an ECS service for a Hello world application

Creating an ECS Service for a Hello world application using the `tutum/hello-world` Docker image is discussed in detail in Chapter 2, *Networking*. In this section, we shall create a `hello-world` cluster consisting of a `hello-world-service` service with three tasks for a `tutum/hello-world` Docker image. To create the cluster, service, and task definition, use the same procedure as in Chapter 2, *Networking* which is as follows:

1. Create a Container Definition, `hello-world`, for the `tutum/hello-world` Docker image

2. Create a task definition, `hello-world-task-definition`
3. Create a service, `hello-world-service`
4. Create a cluster, `hello-world`

The procedure is the same as in `Chapter 2`, *Networking*, except for a few differences. Define the service with three tasks instead of the default one task:

- Click on **Edit** in the **Define your service** section, as shown in the following screenshot:

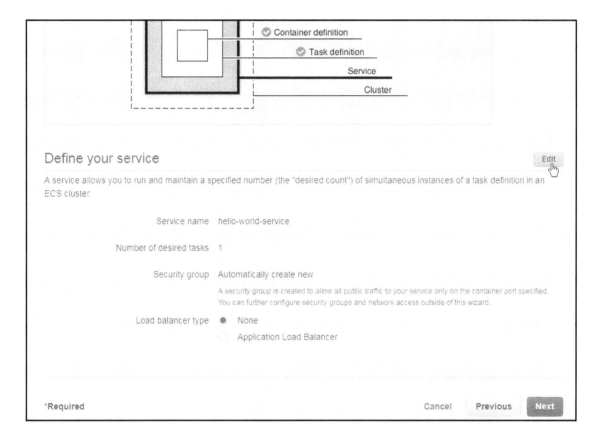

- In the **Set up service: hello-world-service** dialog, set the **Number of desired tasks** to 3, as shown here. Click on **Save**:

- With the **Number of desired tasks** set to **3**, click on **Next** in **Define your service**, as shown here:

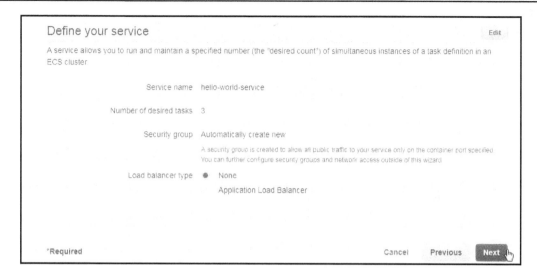

- In **Configure your cluster**, specify the **Cluster name** as **hello-world**, as shown here. The other settings, which include **VPC ID** and **Subnets**, are not modifiable. Click on **Next**:

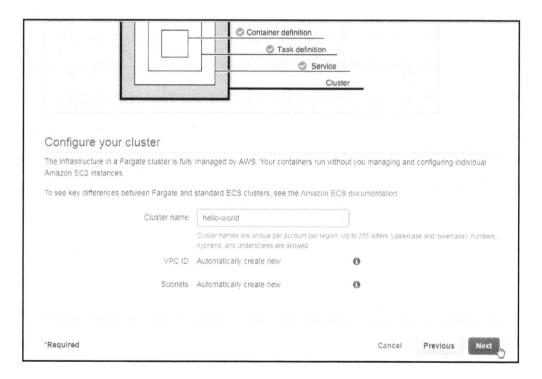

- Review the **Container definition**, **Task definition**, **Service**, and **Cluster** in **Review**, as shown here. An **Edit** button is provided to modify each of these. Click on **Create** to create the ECS objects, as shown here:

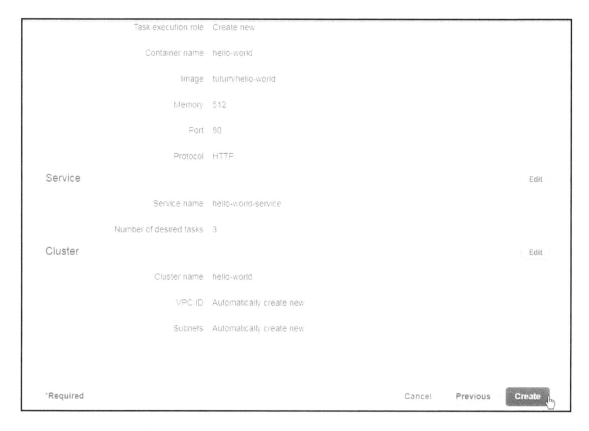

- The **Launch Status** should indicate that all ECS resources have been created, as indicated by the **complete** status shown here. Click on **View service**:

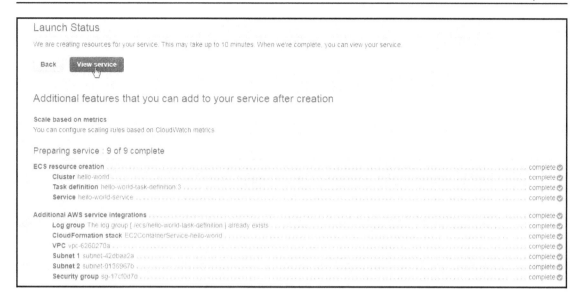

- A service gets created, as shown here. The **Service name**, **Cluster**, **Status**, **Task definition**, **Launch type**, **Platform version**, **Service role**, **Desired count**, **Pending count**, and **Running count** are listed in the service summary. The **Details** tab lists the **Load Balancing** and **Network Access**:

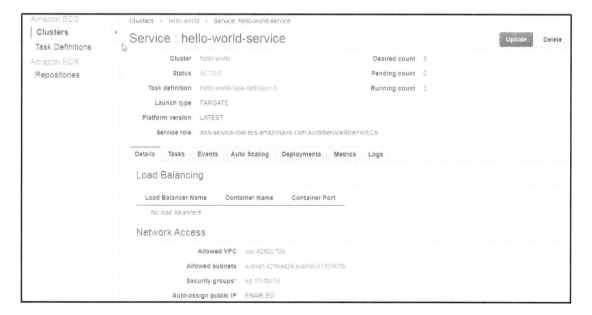

- Select the **Tasks** tab to list the tasks. The **Last status** column lists the task status, which could initially be **PENDING**. Click on the Refresh button periodically to refresh the task status. When all tasks have started running, the **Last status** becomes **RUNNING**, as shown here:

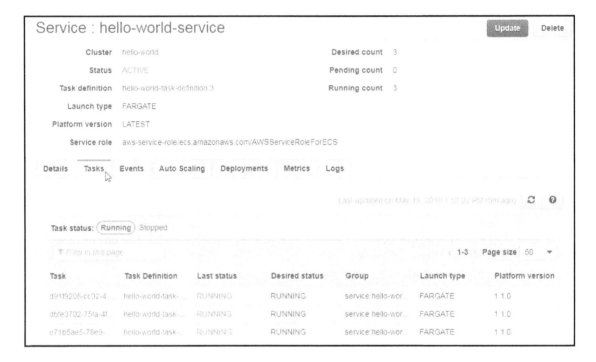

Types of auto scaling

Two kinds of auto scaling policies are defined:

- Target tracking scaling policies
- Step scaling policies

We shall discuss these two kinds of auto scaling policy next, before demonstrating the use of auto scaling.

Target tracking scaling policies

The target being referred to is a target value for a specific metric that CloudWatch metrics monitor. The two ECS metrics CloudWatch monitors are CPU utilization and memory utilization. With target tracking scaling policies, the number of tasks is increased or decreased with the objective that the target value of a metric is kept. It may not be feasible to keep the precise target value of a metric because the number of tasks are increased/decreased in increments/decrements of 1. The metric is kept at the precise configured target value or close to the target value. A target tracking scaling policy itself adjusts itself to the fluctuations in a metric value to avoid rapid fluctuations in the number of tasks. For high application availability, a service scales out faster than it scales in, as fewer tasks hamper application availability while extra tasks do not. Multiple target tracking scaling policies may be set concurrently and the service is scaled to fulfill the scaling policy that effects the greatest increase in task capacity. Increases in CPU or memory utilization are indicators that the application is in need of more tasks and the service scales out if a target metric is exceeded. Sufficient metric data is a prerequisite for a scaling policy to scale. If insufficient data is available, the scaling policy does not scale the number of tasks. To scale if insufficient data is available, a step scaling policy should be used, which is discussed next.

Step scaling policies

In the *Target tracking scaling policies* section, it is mentioned that if insufficient data is available, step scaling policies could be used. To elaborate on this, a CloudWatch alarm could be set to be invoked when a metric state is INSUFFICIENT_DATA. Such a policy is called a Step Scaling Policy. All step scaling policies make use of CloudWatch alarms. CloudWatch alarms can be set to be invoked when a specific CloudWatch metric (CPU utilization or memory utilization) exceeds or goes below a set threshold. As an example, during high use of an application, these metrics are likely to increase and CloudWatch alarms could be set to increase the number of tasks. Similarly, during times of low application load, these metrics decrease in value and CloudWatch alarms could be set to decrease the number of tasks.

Service auto scaling, target tracking auto scaling, or step auto scaling, could modify a services's desired count.

Configuring an auto scaling policy

Auto scaling is not configured by default:

- To configure auto scaling, click on the **Update** button, which is shown in the preceding screenshot, for the service that is to be auto scaled. The **Update Service** wizard gets started, as shown in the following screenshot.
- In the **Configure service** page, the settings are not to be modified unless the **Desired number of tasks** (3) needs to be updated. Click on **Next step**.
- In **Configure network**, we don't need to make any modifications. Click on **Next step**.
- In the **Service auto scaling** page, select the **Service auto scaling** option **Configure Service auto scaling to adjust your service's desired count**, as shown here:

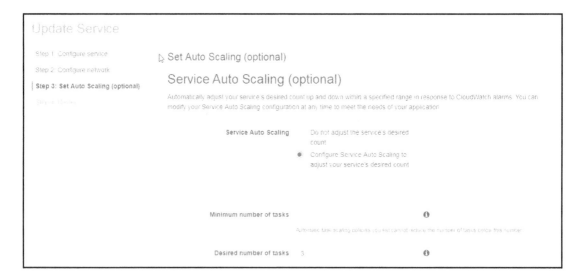

We shall discuss configuring a step auto scaling policy next. Configuring step auto scaling involves the following sequence:

1. Define the range for the number of tasks within which the cluster is to be scaled
2. Add an auto scaling policy
3. Define a CloudWatch alarm as a threshold to apply the scaling policy
4. Define a scaling action to take if the alarm threshold is exceeded

We shall discuss configuring each of these next.

Defining the range of tasks

Specify the **Minimum number of tasks** (1), and the **Maximum number of tasks** (5), as shown in the following screenshot. The number of tasks specified in the example configuration is arbitrary but the maximum number of tasks must be the same or more than the desired number of tasks, and the minimum number of tasks must be the same or less than the desired number of tasks:

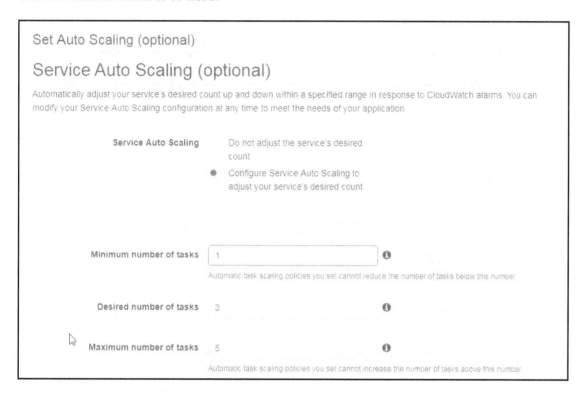

Setting the number of tasks (minimum, desired, and maximum) does not, by itself, configure auto scaling; it only specifies the range in which the number of tasks may fluctuate with load fluctuations. An auto scaling policy also needs to be added.

Adding an auto scaling policy

To add a scaling policy, click on **Add scaling policy**, as shown in the following screenshot:

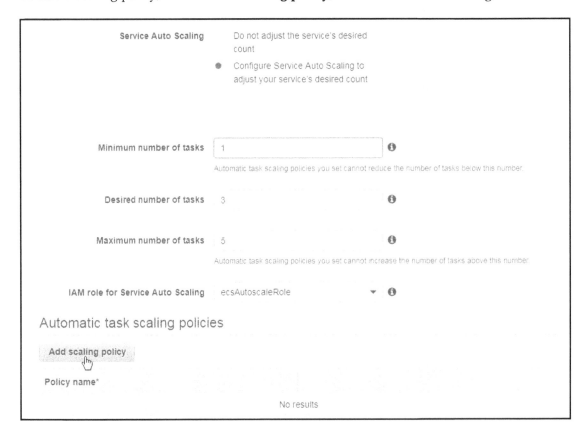

An **Add policy** dialog gets started, as shown in the preceding screenshot.

Next, we shall discuss configuring a step auto scaling policy.

Adding a step scaling policy

- In **Add Policy**, select **Scaling policy type** as **Step scaling**, as shown in the following screenshot.

- Specify a **Policy name** (`AutoScaler`):

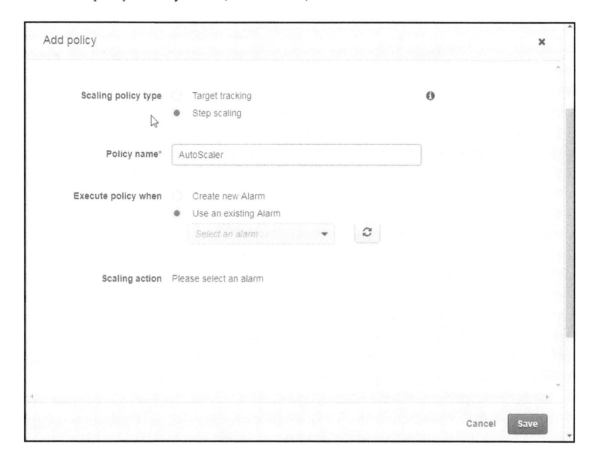

- In **Execute policy when**, select **Create new Alarm**, as shown here. The **Use an existing Alarm** option is also provided if an existing alarm could be used:

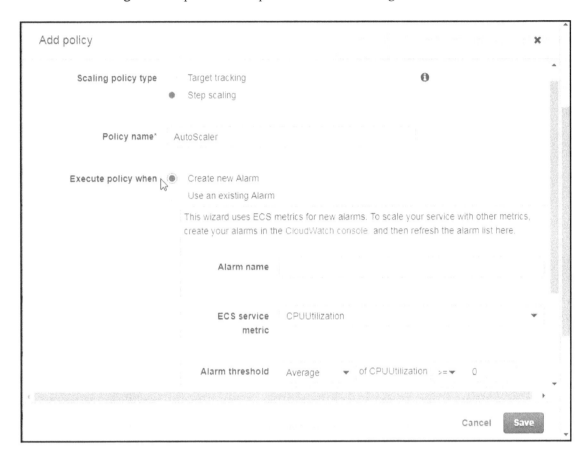

Creating a CloudWatch alarm

In this section, we shall discuss creating a CloudWatch alarm:

- Specify an **Alarm name**, as shown in the following screenshot.
- For a new alarm, ECS metrics are used for the CloudWatch alarm. To use other metrics for auto scaling, create an alarm in the CloudWatch console and select the alarm within **Add policy** with **Use an existing Alarm**. Only two ECS metrics are available for configuring a new alarm in **Add policy**: **CPUUtilization** and **MemorUtilization**. Select **CPUUtilization**.

- The alarm threshold specifies when the auto scaling policy is to be applied. An example of auto scaling is to scale the tasks when **MemoryUtilization** exceeds 256 MB. Different measures are available for defining the alarm threshold. The different alarm threshold measures are Average, Minimum, Maximum, Sum, and Data samples. As an example, select **Maximum**.
- Because the ECS service metric is selected as **CPUUtilization**, the comparison operators (<,<=,>,>=) are defined on CPUUtilization. Select **>=** as an example.
- Specify a value (0.1) for the comparison.
- Specify the number of consecutive periods after which the **Alarm threshold** would have been exceeded and the auto scaling policy should be applied as 1. A period definition is not fixed and different options to define a period are **1 minute**, **5 minutes**, **15 minutes**, and **1 hour**. The lower the frequency value, the faster the response to resource utilization fluctuations would be. Select **1 minute** as an example. Click on **Save**, as shown in the following screenshot:

A CloudWatch alarm for the auto scaling policy has now been defined.

Configuring a scaling action

Next, configure a scaling action for which three options are available: **Add**, **Set to** and **Remove**:

- Select **Add** to add a specified number of tasks when the alarm threshold is exceeded. By alarm threshold exceeded, it does not always imply that some value for a metric has been exceeded, but implies that the comparison used in the alarm threshold has been exceeded. The comparison itself could be a less than (<) comparison.
- Specify the number of **tasks** to add as 1. Alternatively, a percentage of tasks may be added by selecting **percent**. The complete scaling is shown next.
- Multiple scaling actions may be defined with **Add**.
- Specify a **Cooldown period** (300 is the default) between scaling actions. The cooldown period is relevant if multiple scaling actions are used and we have not used multiple scaling actions. Click on **Save**:

- An auto scaling policy (**AutoScaler**), including the range of tasks, gets defined as shown here. Click on **Next step**:

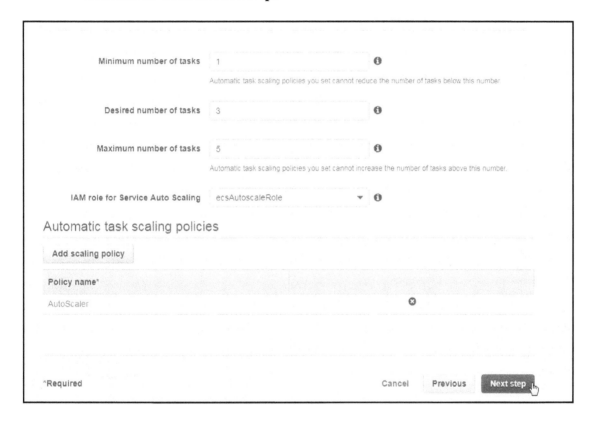

- In **Review**, click on **Update Service**, as shown in the following screenshot:

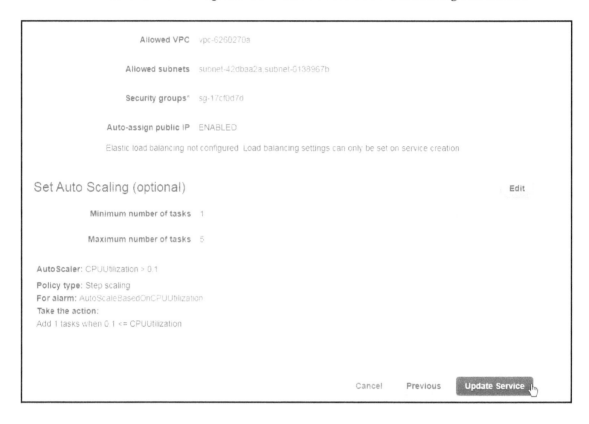

Launch Status indicates that the service has been updated, as shown in the following screenshot:

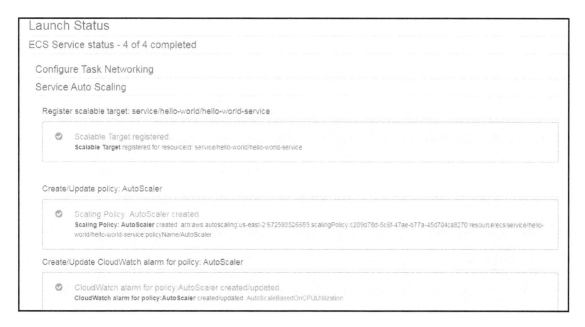

The following configurations get applied:

- Scalable target gets registered
- The scaling policy `AutoScaler` gets created
- CloudWatch alarm for scaling policy gets created/updated

Click on **View Service**, as shown in the following screenshot:

The updated service is shown here. Select the **auto scaling** tab to display the auto scaling policy added. The auto scaling tab lists the **Minimum tasks**, **Maximum tasks**, **AutoScaler**, **Policy type**, CloudWatch alarm, and Scaling action:

The **Events** tab lists the events for the service, as shown here. As indicated by an event entry, the service has started three tasks and reached a steady state:

An auto scaling policy has been configured. Select the **Tasks** tab and three tasks are running as before, as shown here. The number of tasks is still three, the same as before adding the auto scaling policy, because the service does not need to be auto scaled and the three tasks are able to handle the client load:

Demonstrating the use of auto scaling

In this section, we shall demonstrate the use of auto scaling by adding an extra load to the Hello world service.

- Invoke the service using the public IP of one of the tasks; the public IP may be obtained from a task's details, as shown in the following screenshot:

- First, invoke the service in one browser only. The Hello world application gets invoked and the service response gets displayed in the browser, as shown in the following screenshot:

- To increase the load, invoke the same Hello world application multiple times using the curl tool. Run the following command on a Windows Command line:

```
curl http://18.191.95.171/?[1-20]
```

- An internal load balancer automatically distributes the client load among the tasks in a service, regardless of which task is invoked by a client. An external load balancer may also be configured, as discussed in a later chapter. As the client load on the Hello world service is increased, the number of tasks also gets increased if the existing number of tasks are not able to handle the load. As shown here, the number of running tasks has increased to four:

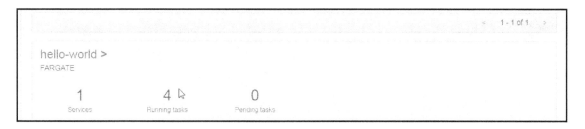

- Increase the load on the service still further with the following curl command:

```
curl http://18.191.95.171/?[1-1000]
```

- As shown here, the number of tasks has increased to five, which is the maximum number of tasks that the auto scaler is able to scale to, as specified in the auto scaling configuration for the service:

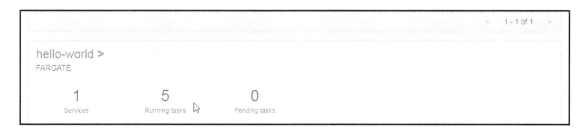

- The five running tasks are listed in the **Tasks** tab for the service, as shown here:

Exploring CloudWatch metrics and Logs

In this section, we shall explore the CloudWatch metrics and logs generated by the ECS service and find log events for the CloudWatch alarm threshold being exceeded:

- Open the CloudWatch console as shown here. The alarm summary for the `AutoScaleCPUUtilization` gets displayed in a graph.
- Click on **Browse Metrics** to browse metrics:

- Select Alarms in the margin. The **AutoScaleBasedOnCPUUtilization** alarm used as a threshold for auto scaling gets listed, as shown in the following screenshot. The alarm state is ALARM when the alarm threshold is exceeded.

  The **AutoScaleBasedOnCPUUtilization** alarm details and graph get displayed. The two spikes in CPU utilization in the graph indicate that the alarm threshold has been exceeded, which applies the auto scaling to add one task each time the alarm threshold is exceeded. The first spike in the graph is for when the load is increased slightly, and the second spike is for when the load is increased to a greater extent:

- When the load on the ECS service is reduced, the alarm state becomes **OK**. Reducing client load does not by itself reduce the number of running tasks. The scaling action used as an example only scales up the tasks if client load increases. Another scaling action would need to be added to scale down tasks on client load reduction. In the **History** tab, two instances of auto scaling action are listed, as shown in the following screenshot:

- The **Desired count** of the service has been updated to 5, in addition to increasing the auto scaling running count to five tasks. The **AutoScaleBasedOnCPUUtilization** alarm may also be accessed from the **auto scaling** tab:

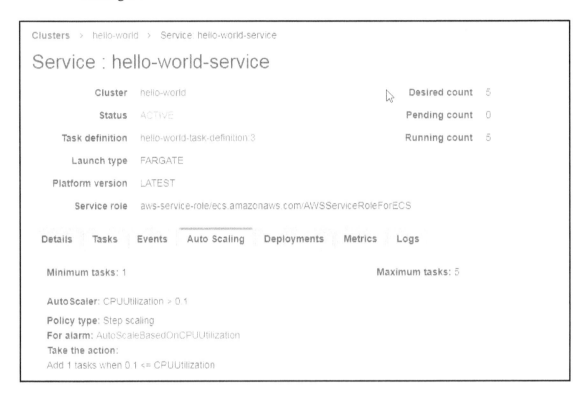

Updating auto scaling policy

The auto scaling policy only scales the number of running (desired) tasks and does not modify the auto scaling policy, which is still set to a range of 1-5 tasks. The service may be updated to modify any or all of the minimum number of tasks, desired count, maximum number of tasks, and scaling action for auto scaling. In this section, we shall discuss updating the auto scaling configuration:

- Click on **Update** for the service as before. The **Desired number of tasks** is set to 5, as shown here, when auto scaling is performed:

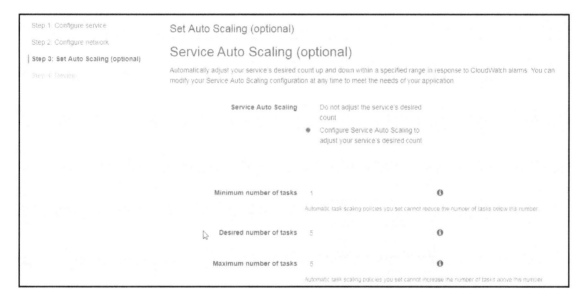

- Reduce the **Desired number of tasks** to 3, as shown here.

- To modify the scaling policy, click on the **AutoScaler** link, as shown here:

- In **Edit policy**, select **Use an existing** policy and select the
  AutoScaleBasedOnCPUUtilization policy. The scaling action does not have to
  be performed when the alarm threshold is breached. Modify the scaling action to
  Add 1 tasks when 0.9<=CPUUtilization, as shown here. The alarm threshold
  is CPUUtilization> 0.1 for 60 seconds, while the scaling action is performed
  when CPUUtilization>=0.9. The AutoScaler policy runs each time the
  CloudWatch alarm threshold is breached, but the scaling action is performed
  only when CPUUtilization>=0.9. Click on **Save**:

- The minimum and maximum number of tasks has not been modified and is still **1** and **5** respectively. Click on **Next step**, and then click on **Update Service**, as shown here:

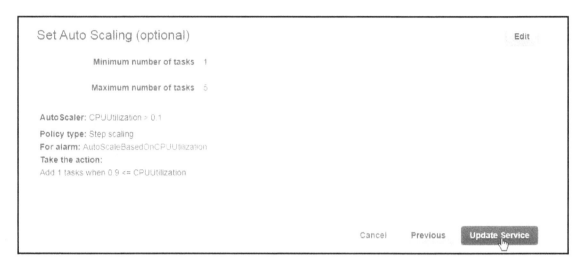

- The old auto scaling policy gets deleted and a new auto scaling policy gets created, as shown here. The scalable target is the same as before:

- The CloudWatch alarm gets updated. Click on **View Service**. The **Running count** and **Desired count** of the service are both **3**, as shown here. The scaling action has been updated to **Add 1 tasks when 0.9 <= CPUUtilization**:

- The **Events** tab lists the log events generated by the ECS service, as shown here. The number of running tasks had increased to five when the client load was increased. But, when the client load is removed and the scaling policy updated, the number of running tasks becomes three again. As listed in an event, the service has stopped two running tasks:

Event Id	Event Time	Message
82e8a398-934c-48a3-80aa-5277e6d66f93	2018-05-19 18:14:12 -0700	service hello-world-service has reached a steady state.
36a282cd-dcaa-4449-9263-d87e6c09826c	2018-05-19 18:14:02 -0700	service hello-world-service has stopped 2 running tasks: task d91f9208-cc02-434b-b9a0-483d463904b1 task dbfe3702-75fa-4fc4-a2ea-519f72550c23
ca3447eb-b0fe-43e4-9252-ac84ad6fb7ad	2018-05-19 17:35:13 -0700	service hello-world-service has reached a steady state.
fc0fcc1a-8ab1-404d-978a-fbe4f73e730b	2018-05-19 17:34:45 -0700	service hello-world-service has started 1 tasks: task abc17cdf-111b-469f-8c91-8a4a2d54adf6.
b0175347-c206-4c8e-acc6-6d2c6449e7dc	2018-05-19 17:34:41 -0700	Message: Successfully set desired count to 5. Change successfully fulfilled by ecs. Cause: monitor alarm AutoScaleBasedOnCPUUtilization in state ALARM triggered policy AutoScaler
fed0febe-6956-4940-9634-795861ffb1a9	2018-05-19 17:25:04 -0700	service hello-world-service has reached a steady state.
9730b827-2352-457c-a362-f11134e380e5	2018-05-19 17:24:45 -0700	service hello-world-service has started 1 tasks: task 2e576389-3d48-4a13-bba9-caea301fb746
6176175c-aa20-4741-95d0-2b2ab157ae05	2018-05-19 17:24:41 -0700	Message: Successfully set desired count to 4. Change successfully fulfilled by ecs. Cause: monitor alarm AutoScaleBasedOnCPUUtilization in state ALARM triggered policy AutoScaler
b2da6faa-cf1c-49e3-903d-808b84438a52	2018-05-19 13:48:46 -0700	service hello-world-service has reached a steady state.
468b7da9-ea52-423d-abef-a25ea4874fc5	2018-05-19 13:48:11 -0700	service hello-world-service has started 3 tasks: task e71b5ae5-78e9-46b5-90a6-a36d1ae0396a task d91f9208-cc02-434b-b9a0-483d463904b1 task dbfe3702-75fa-4fc4-a2ea-519f72550c23

Initially, one task is started. When the alarm threshold is breached for the first time, the scaling action is performed to set the desired count for the maximum number of tasks to four, as indicated by one of the log messages. The number of running tasks increases to four. When the load is increased still further, the alarm threshold is breached for the second time and a scaling action is performed to set the desired count for the maximum number of tasks to five. The number of running tasks increases to five. When the client load is removed and the service is updated to modify the desired count to three, two of the running tasks get stopped, as indicated by another event message.

Summary

In this chapter, we introduced the ECS auto scaling service, as used with the Fargate launch type. Configuring auto scaling involves setting a range (minimum and maximum) for the number of tasks within which the auto scaling gets applied. Configuring auto scaling also requires an auto scaling policy, consisting of a CloudWatch alarm threshold for running the auto scaling policy, and one or more scaling actions to perform each time the auto scaling policy runs. In the next chapter, we shall discuss using an IAM user with Fargate.

Using IAM

5

Amazon ECS is integrated with, and makes use of, several other AWS services, including Elastic Load Balancing and EC2. ECS makes use of service-linked roles, which are special types of roles associated with a service to provide access to the required AWS services without additional configuration. ECS makes use of the `AWSServiceRoleForECS` role to access other AWS services for managing EC2 network interfaces, registering/deregistering instances from a load balancer, and registering targets. A root user does not require any additional configuration to be able to use ECS with Fargate.

Problem: An IAM user does not have permission to create or modify ECS resources or invoke the ECS API by default. An IAM user also does not have permissions to use the ECS Console or the AWS CLI.

Solution: An IAM user must be granted permission to create the `AWSServiceRoleForECS` role. An IAM policy may be created and associated with an IAM user to grant the requisite permissions to use some of the other AWS services. Some of the AWS services that may be required to run Amazon ECS include:

- Calls to Amazon ECR to pull Docker images
- Calls to CloudWatch Logs to store container logs

The `AmazonECSTaskExecutionRolePolicy` policy is provided to grant permissions for using the aforementioned ECS services.

Some of the Elastic Load Balancing permissions are not included in the `AWSServiceRoleForECS` role and an IAM policy may be required to be added to use Elastic Load Balancing. The `AmazonEC2ContainerServiceRole` policy may be used to register/deregister container instances with load balancers. The service auto scaling IAM role (`ecsAutoscaleRole`) is required to configure auto scaling. An IAM user must add `ecsAutoscaleRole`, which must include the `AmazonEC2ContainerServiceAutoscaleRole` policy. To be able to use IAM roles for tasks, the Amazon EC2 Container Service Task Role policy must be added.

The `AmazonEC2ContainerServiceforEC2Role` policy is not required with the Fargate launch type, as it is provided for the EC2 launch type only.

In this chapter, we will learn about the following:

- Creating an IAM User
- Adding a custom policy for Elastic Load Balancing
- Logging in as the IAM User

The only prerequisite is an AWS account.

Creating an IAM user

To create an IAM user, log in as the root user and access the IAM Console at `https://console.aws.amazon.com/iam`:

- Select users in the left-hand menu and click on **Add user**, as shown in the following screenshot:

- The **Add user** wizard gets launched, as shown next. First, specify the **User name** (`dvohra`).
- Select the **AWS Management Console** access option, which enables a password that allows the IAM user to log in to the Console:

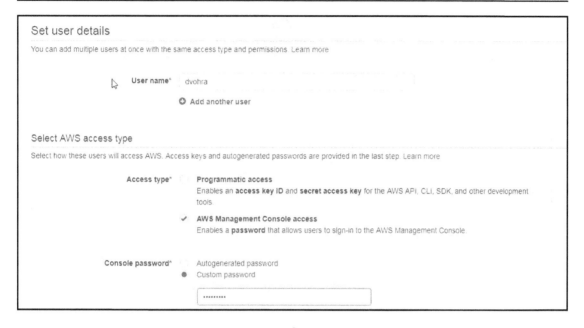

- For **Console Password**, select the **Custom password** option and specify a password in the field provided. Select the **Require password reset** option, which requires a user to create a new password at the next login. Users are automatically granted the `IAMUserChangePassword` policy, which allows a user to change their password. Click on **Next**.
- Next, configure permissions. Click on **Attach existing policy directly**, as shown here:

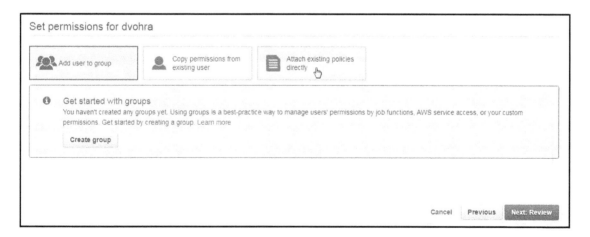

- In the **Policy type** filter, search for **ECS** and select the two policies listed next. `AmazonECS_FullAccess` provides administrative access to Amazon ECS resources. `AmazonECSTaskExecutionRole` provides access to the other AWS resources that are required by ECS:

- Search for the **Config** in **Policy type** filter and select the **AWS Config** policies shown next. Click on **Next**:

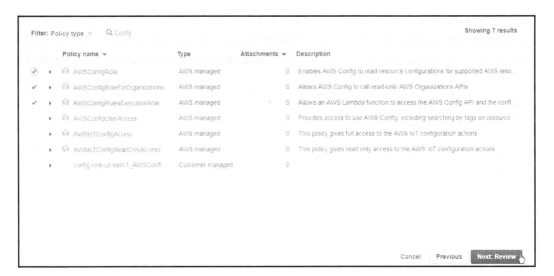

In **Review**, review the **Permissions Summary**, and the **IAMUserChangePassword** policy should also be listed. Click on **Create user**. An IAM user gets added, as indicated by the **Success** message. This IAM user gets listed in the users table as shown here. We shall use the IAM user with Amazon Fargate in subsequent chapters:

Adding a custom policy for Elastic Load Balancing

The ECS policies available and selected do not include some permissions that are required when creating an Elastic Load Balancer for an ECS service. We need to add a custom policy to the IAM user so that the IAM user is able to configure an Elastic Load Balancer. The following custom policy adds all the `elasticloadbalancing` permissions:

```
{
  "Version": "2012-10-17",
  "Statement":[{
    "Effect": "Allow",
    "Action": ""elasticloadbalancing:*",
    "Resource": "*"
  }]
}
```

The custom policy may be added using one of the following options:

- Create a custom policy prior to creating the user
- Add an inline policy after a user has been created

We shall discuss the second option:

- To add the custom policy as an inline policy, click on the IAM user link for IAM user **dvohra** (or another user) in the **Users** table. The IAM user detail gets displayed.
- With the **Permissions** tab selected, click on **Add inline policy**, as shown in the following screenshot:

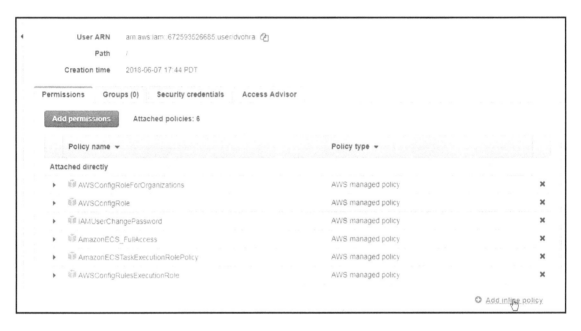

- The **Create policy** wizard gets started. Select the **JSON** tab and copy and paste the custom policy listed earlier, as shown in the following screenshot:

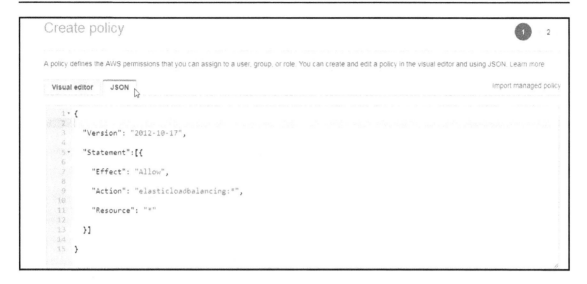

- Click on **Review policy**. Specify a policy **Name**, as shown next.
- Click on **Create policy**, as shown in the following screenshot:

- The custom policy gets added to the IAM user permissions, as shown in the following screenshot:

Logging in as the IAM user

Next, having created an IAM user, log in as the IAM user to use Amazon Fargate:

- To be able to log in as the IAM user just created, first **Sign Out** as the root user:

- To sign in to the Console, copy the **Console login link https://123456789.signin.aws.amazon.com/console**, which would be different for different users, as shown here. The link listed is just an example link and cannot be used to log in:

- Open a web browser with the Console login link. The Account ID is pre-specified in the login form (not shown in following screenshot). Specify the IAM user name and password and click on **Sign In**, as shown in the following screenshot:

- Next, the form to change the password is provided. Because the option to change the password at first login was selected, the IAM user must configure a new password. Click on **Confirm password change**. The IAM user gets logged in as shown in the following screenshot.
- Select the **Elastic Container Service** to create an ECS service, as shown in the following screenshot:

Summary

In this chapter, we discussed configuring an IAM user for ECS. The root user does not require any permission configurations and has access to the ECS resources, ECS Console, ECS API, and all the required AWS services. If an IAM user is to be used with ECS, the required IAM policies must be added to the IAM user. To use ECS with Elastic Load Balancing, a custom policy must be added. In the next chapter, we shall discuss using an application load balancer with Fargate.

6
Using an Application Load Balancer

While some Docker containers accept TCP client requests, other Docker containers accept client requests on an HTTP path. As demonstrated in Chapter 2, *Networking,* an HTTP request to a Hello World application task could be made on the public IP address exposed by the Hello World task. An ECS service includes built-in internal load balancing to distribute client traffic between the tasks in a service.

Problem : Each task in an ECS service with Fargate launch is associated with an ENI and a public IP. When an application is scaled up to run multiple tasks, multiple ENIs are created, and each task must be accessed on its public IP address.

Although internal load balancing is provided, no provision is included to balance client traffic externally between the different tasks' IP addresses. A single task could receive an inordinate number of client requests, while another task could receive relatively fewer client requests, or even none, which would result in an imbalance in the routing of the external client load, as illustrated in the following diagram. If the task (or tasks) to which the client load is directed fails, the application fails to serve any client requests. High availability of an ECS hosted application is not provided. Exposing containers directly to the public is not the best security practice.

It is always recommended to put them behind an ELB to allow network traffic control in terms of security.

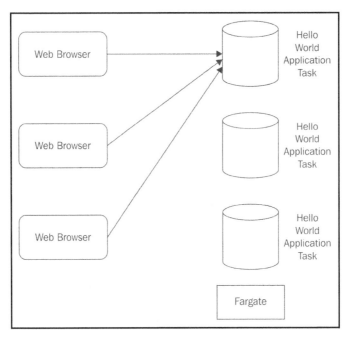

Solution: With an HTTP protocol application such as the Hello World application, an EC2 **Application Load Balancer** may be used to route HTTP client requests to the different tasks in an ECS service. An **Application Load Balancer** is an external load balancer that exposes a public DNS, and all client requests are directed to the single public DNS. The **Application Load Balancer** balances the client load between the application's tasks, providing the high availability of an ECS-hosted application as a result, as illustrated in the following diagram. Even if one of the tasks were to fail, the **Application Load Balancer** would direct the client traffic to tasks that are still available:

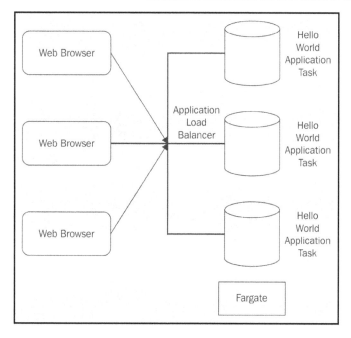

In this chapter, we will learn about the following:

- Creating an application load balancer
- Creating a task definition
- Creating a service
- Configuring an application load balancer
- Invoking the Hello World application
- Stopping tasks and deleting a load balancer

The only prerequisite is having an AWS account.

Creating an application load balancer

The following procedure is used to configure a Fargate ECS service with an application load Balancer:

1. Create an application load balancer
2. Create a task definition

3. Create a service
4. Configure the application load balancer with the service
5. Invoke the service

First, we shall create an application load balancer:

1. Open the EC2 Console in a browser by going to `https://console.aws.amazon.com/ec2`, and select **Load Balancing | Load Balancers**.

2. Click on **Create Load Balancer**, as shown in the following screenshot:

3. In **Select load balancer type**, click on **Create** for the **Application Load Balancer**, as shown in the following screenshot. An application load balancer is used for **HTTP/HTTPS** request protocols.

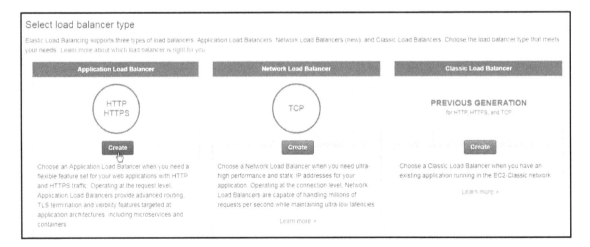

4. In **Configure Load Balancer**, specify a load balancer name (hello-world-lb) in the **Basic Configuration**, as shown in the following screenshot, and select **internet-facing** as the **Scheme**. Only a-z, A-Z, 0-9, and hyphens may be used in the load balancer name.

5. Select **ipv4** as the **IP address type**.

6. In the **Listeners** section, a listener is configured with **HTTP** as the **Load Balancer Protocol**, and 80 as the **Load Balancer Port**:

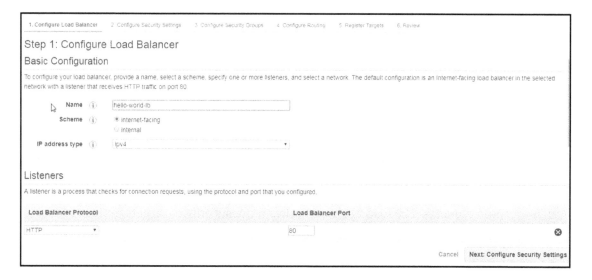

7. Scroll down and choose a VPC. Select at least the availability zones to which the load balancer is going to route traffic. Click on **Next**.

8. The **Configure Security Settings** page will then be displayed for an **HTTPS** listener. If the load balancer should use an HTTPS protocol listener, that should be configured on the previous screen in the **Listeners** section, and the security settings should be configured on the **Configure Security Settings** page. Because we are only using an **HTTP** listener, we don't need to configure any security settings. Click on **Next**.

9. Configure **Security Groups** for the load balancer. Select **Create a new security group** and select the default **Security group name**, which is also shown in the following screenshot.

10. Select **All traffic** as the **Type**, a **Protocol** of **All**,
    Port Range of **0-65535**, and **Custom** as the **Source**, with CIDR as default routes
    for IPv4 and IPv6 (**0.0.0.0/0, ::/0**). Click on **Next**:

11. In **Configure Routing**, configure a target group to which the load balancer will
    route requests. The load balancer routes requests only to targets in the
    configured target group. Select the **New Target group** option in **Target group**,
    and specify a **Name** (hello-world-tg), as shown in the following screenshot.

12. Select **HTTP** as the **Protocol** and 80 as the **Port**.

13. Select **ip** as the **Target type** and click on **Next**:

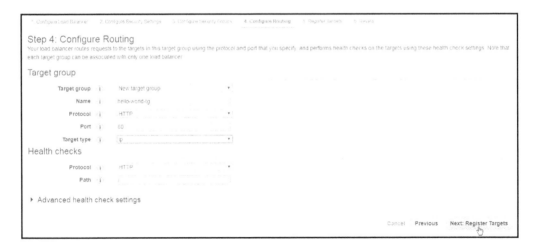

14. With a Target type of ip, targets in the following CIDR blocks may be added: 10.0.0.0/8, 100.64.0.0/10, 172.16.0.0/12, and 192.168.0.0/16.

15. On the **Register Targets** screen (shown in the following screenshot), we won't register targets, as Fargate does that automatically when an ECS service using the application load balancer is created. Click on **Next**:

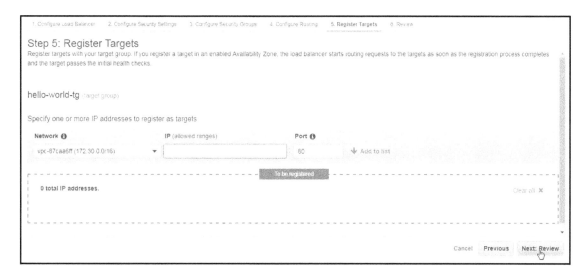

16. Review the configuration for the application load balancer. Click on **Create**, as shown in the following screenshot:

17. The application load balancer gets created, as indicated by the **Load Balancer Creation Status** dialog. Click on **Close**.

18. The `hello-world-lb` load balancer is listed in the load balancer table, as shown in the following screenshot. Initially, the status (**State**) is **provisioning**. Click on **Refresh** to refresh the **State**:

19. When the load balancer becomes available, its **State** becomes **active**, as shown in the following screenshot:

20. A target group, `hello-world-tg`, gets created, also shown in the following screenshot:

21. Select the **Targets** tab and no targets should initially be listed, as none have been configured yet.

Creating a task definition

In this section, we will create a task definition for a `hello-world` application using the `tutum/hello-world` Docker image. Another Docker image that exposes a HTTP port may also be used, but not all Docker images may be used. As an unsuitable example, the MySQL database Docker image, `mysql`, cannot be used with an application load balancer, as it exposes a TCP port, `3306`. For an ECS task that exposes a TCP port, a network load balancer should be used.

1. To create a new task definition, select **Task Definitions** in the ECS console, as shown in the following screenshot:

2. In **Task Definitions**, click on **Create new Task Definition**, as shown in the following screenshot:

3. In **Create new Task Definition**, select **Fargate** as the launch type compatibility, as shown in the following screenshot. Scroll down and click on **Next step**:

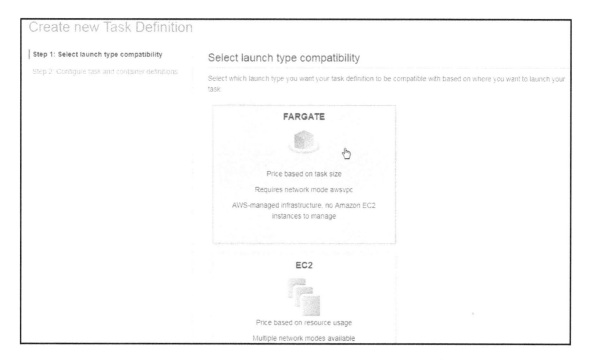

4. In **Configure task and container definitions**, specify a **Task Definition Name** (**hello-world-task-definition**) and select **ecsTaskExecutionRole** as the **Task Role**, as shown in the following screenshot.

5. The **Network Mode** is **awsvpc** for Fargate, and cannot be modified as it is the only one supported, as shown in the following screenshot:

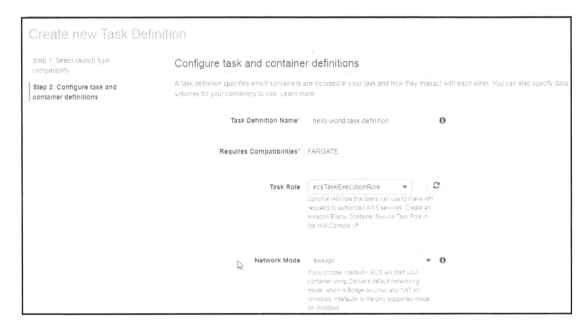

6. Select **excsTaskExecutionRole** as the **Task execution IAM role**, as shown in the following screenshot. This role is required to send container logs to CloudWatch:

7. In **Task size**, select **0.5GB** as the **Task memory**, as shown in the following screenshot. Select **0.25 vCPU** as the **Task CPU**:

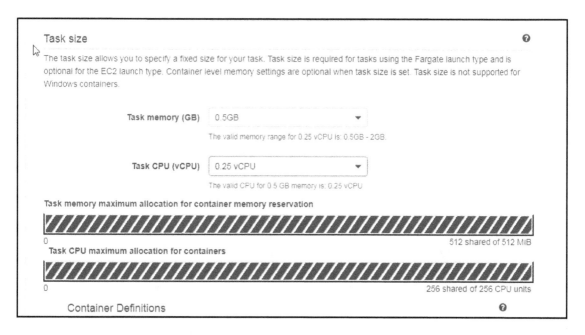

8. To add a container definition, click on **Add container** in **Container Definitions**, as shown in the following screenshot:

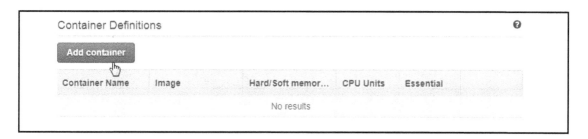

9. In **Add container**, specify **Container name** (hello-world), **Image** (tutum/hello-world), and **Memory Limits**, as shown in the following screenshot:

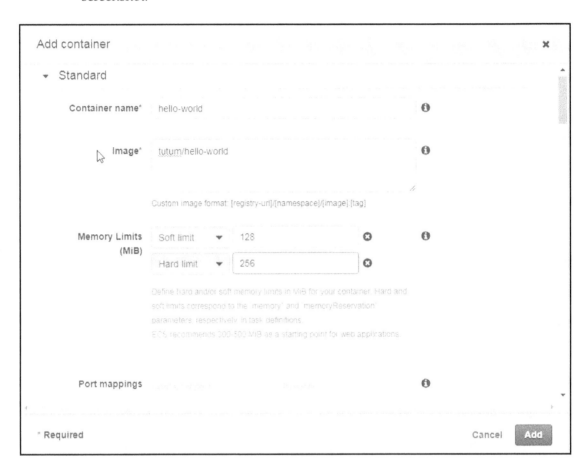

10. Set **Container port** to 80 in **Port mappings,** as shown in the following screenshot:

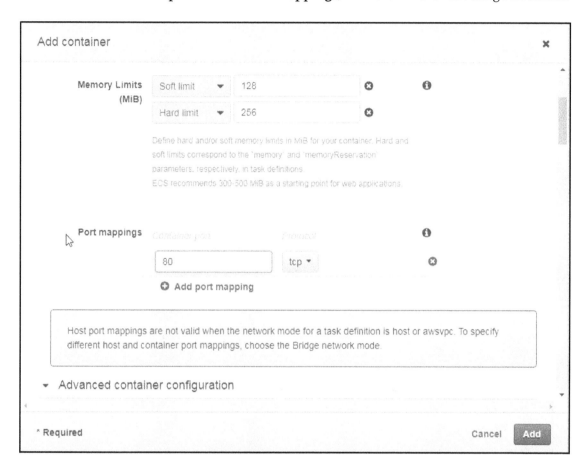

11. In **Advanced container configuration | ENVIRONMENT**, set **CPU units** to 10 and check the **Essential** checkbox, as shown in the following screenshot, as one container in a task must be essential to the running of a task and the hello-world container is the only container, it must be configured as **Essential**:

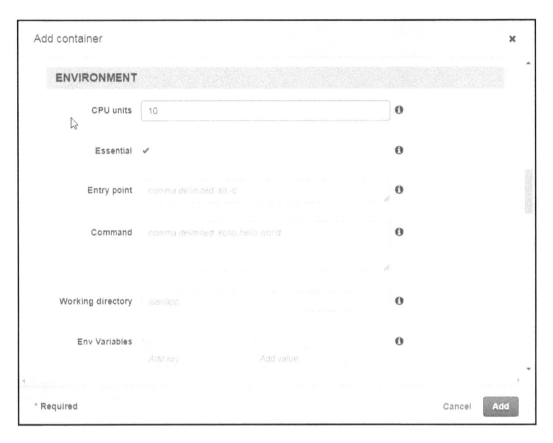

12. After configuring all the container definition settings, click on **Add** in **Add container**. A container definition gets added, as shown in the following screenshot.

13. Click on **Create** to create the task definition, which includes the container definition:

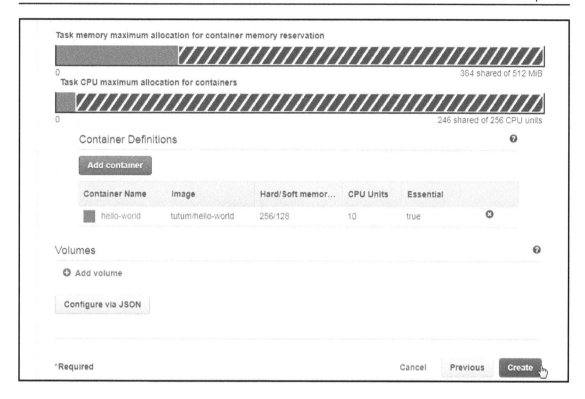

14. The task definition gets created, as shown in the **Launch Status** dialog. Click on **View task definition**, as shown in in the following screenshot:

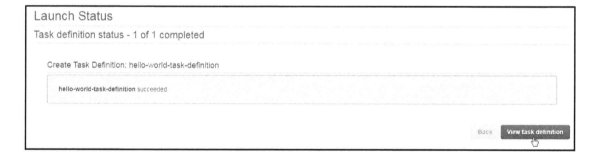

15. A new task definition **Builder** and detailed **JSON** information gets displayed, as shown in the following screenshot. **Requires compatibilities** must be set to **FARGATE**, as shown in the following screenshot:

16. Select **Task Definitions** from the margin navigation. The task definition gets listed in the **Task Definitions** table, as shown in the following screenshot:

Creating a service

A service is an implementation of a task definition, and runs tasks. To create a service, a cluster must be selected.

1. Click on the **default** cluster link, as shown in the following screenshot:

2. Select the **Services** tab and click on **Create**, as shown in the following screenshot:

3. In **Configure service**, select **FARGATE** as the **Launch type** and select the **Task definition** created earlier.

4. Select **LATEST** as the **Platform version**. The default cluster should be listed as selected, because we selected default to start with.

5. Specify a **Service name** (`hello-world-service`) and set **Number of tasks** to **3**, as shown in the following screenshot:

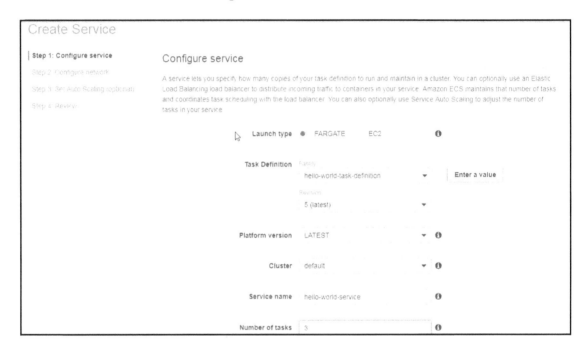

6. Leaving the other settings as their defaults, click on **Next** step.

Configuring an application load balancer

In this section, we shall configure the application load balancer.

1. First, select a **Cluster VPC** and two **Subnets**, as shown in the following screenshot. The VPC should be the same one that the application load balancer was created in. The Security group that gets created is listed. **Auto-assign public IP** must be set to **ENABLED**:

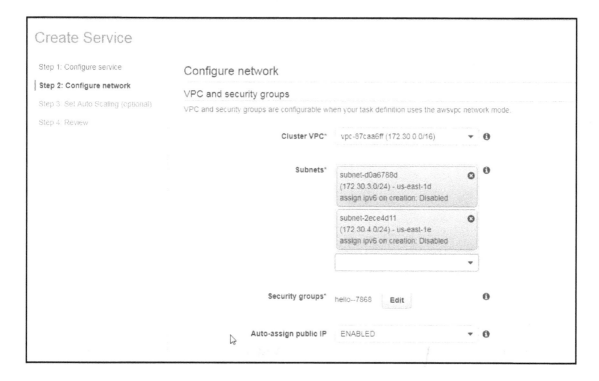

2. In the **Load balancing** section, select **Application Load Balancer** as the **Load balancer type**, as shown in the following screenshot. Select the **Load balancer name** (hello-world-lb) created earlier:

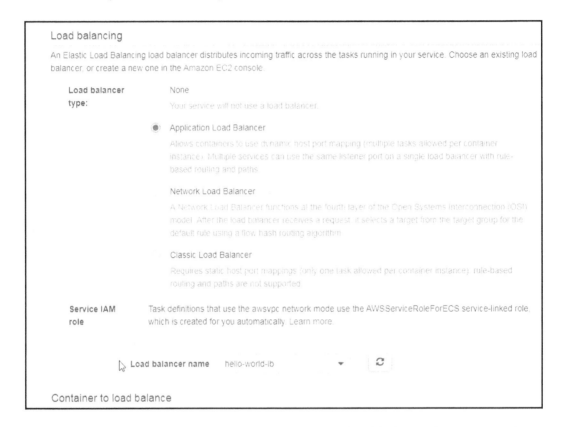

3. In **Container to load balance**, click on **Add to load balancer** for the **Container name:port** to be created as hello-world:80:80, as shown in the following screenshot:

4. Additional fields get displayed to configure the container to load balance. Select **80:HTTP** as the **Listener port**, as shown in the following screenshot.
5. Select **Target group name** as **hello-world-tg**, which is the target group created when the load balancer was created, as shown in the following screenshot.
6. In **Service discovery**, deselect the checkbox **Enable service discovery integration**.
7. Keep the default settings for the other fields and click on **Next step**:

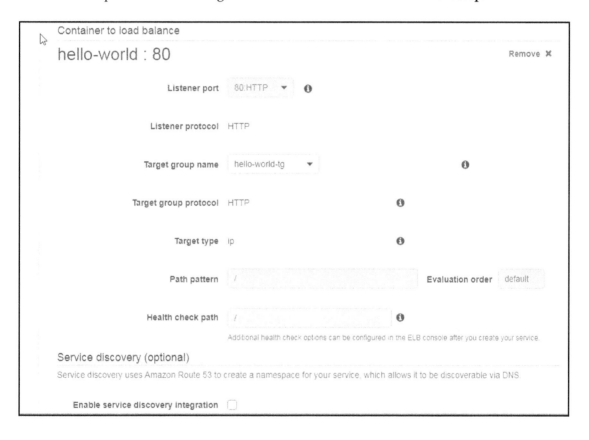

8. In **Set Auto Scaling** (shown in the following screenshot), auto scaling may optionally be configured, but is not required. Click on **Next step** with the default setting of **Do not adjust the service's desired count**:

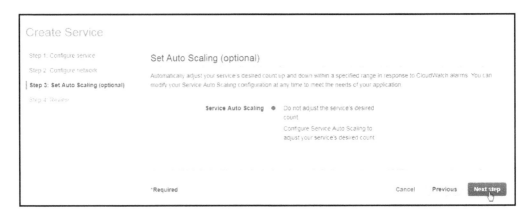

9. In **Review**, click on **Create Service**, as shown in the following screenshot:

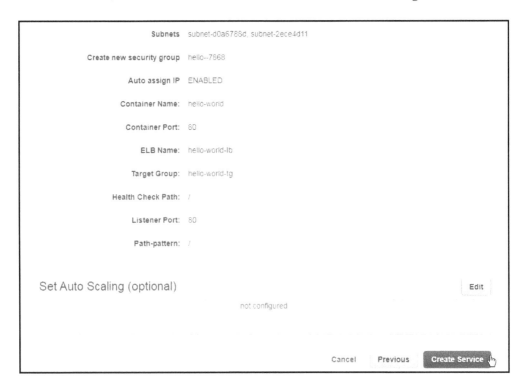

10. As the **Launch Status** dialog shown in the following screenshot indicates, a service gets created:

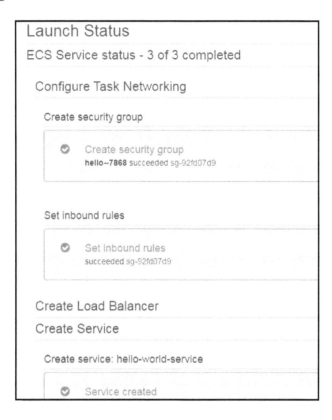

11. Initially, some of the tasks could have a status of **PENDING**. Click on the refresh button to refresh the status. After a while, all the tasks should have a status of **RUNNING**, as shown in the following screenshot:

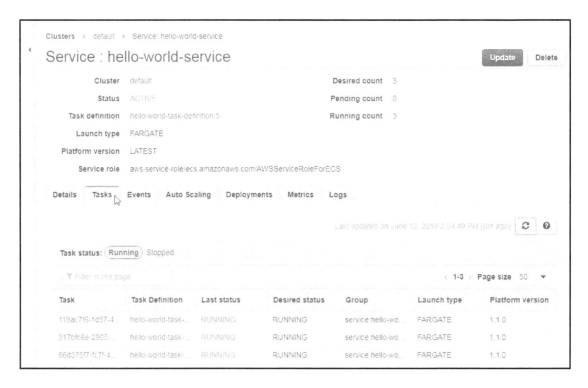

12. The service **Details** tab lists the configuration of load balancing, including the **Target Group Name**, **Container Name**, and **Container Port**, as shown in the following screenshot. The service summary lists a deployment with a **Running count** of 3 for a **Desired count** of 3:

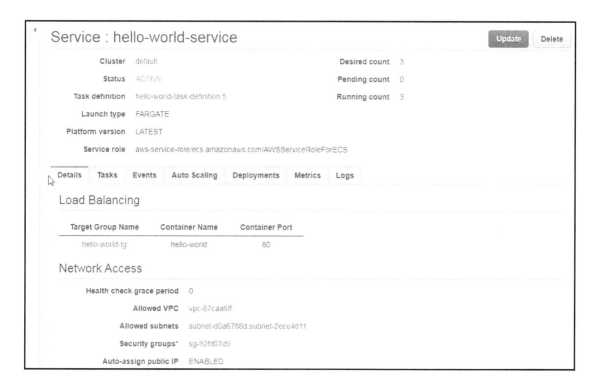

13. **Events** indicates that the service registered 1 target in the target group, as shown in the following screenshot:

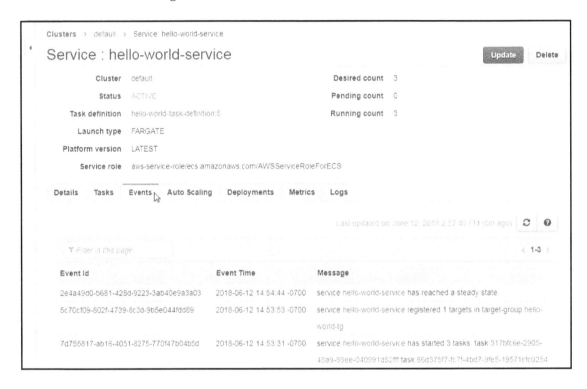

Invoking the Hello World application

To invoke the `hello-world` service in a browser, we will use the public DNS of the application load balancer registered with the service. In the EC2 dashboard, select the **Target Groups** | **hello-world-tg** target group, and then select **Targets**. Initially, when the target group was created, the **Targets** tab did not list any targets. But after creating and configuring the service with the load balancer, the **Targets** tab lists the three IP addresses for the three tasks in the **hello-world-tg** service, as shown in the following screenshot:

Two of the tasks are in one availability zone and the third is in another availability zone, as shown in the following screenshot:

1. Obtain the **DNS name** for the application load balancer from the Load Balancers console, as shown in the following screenshot:

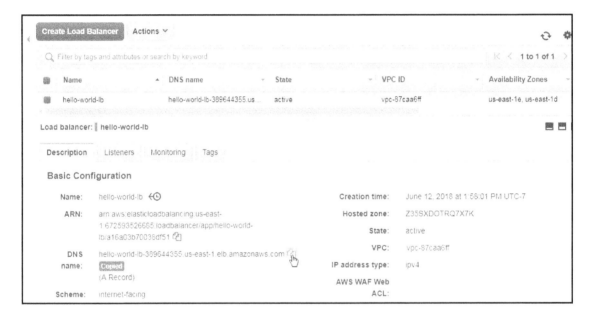

2. Open the DNS name in a browser to invoke the Hello World application, as shown in the following screenshot:

Invoking the DNS name for the load balancer forwards the request to the target group **hello-world-tg**, as indicated in the **Listeners** tab of the load balancer, as shown in the following screenshot:

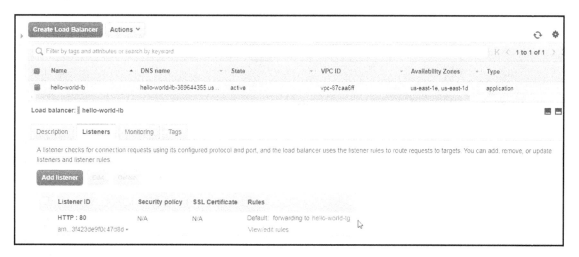

Stopping tasks and deleting a load balancer

The procedure used to stop tasks and delete ECS resources is as follows:

1. Update the service to set Desired count for tasks to 0
2. Stop the tasks
3. Delete the service
4. De-register the task definition revisions

To delete the application load balancer, select the application load balancer in the **Load Balancers** table and select **Actions** | **Delete**, as shown in the following screenshot:

In the **Delete Load Balancer** confirmation dialog, click on **Yes, Delete**. The application load balancer gets deleted as shown in the following screenshot:

Summary

In this chapter, we discussed configuring an ECS service with a Fargate launch type with an application load balancer to balance the HTTP requests for a Hello World service. The application load balancer is designed for HTTP/HTTPS protocol, and cannot be used with TCP protocol. In the next chapter, we will discuss using the Amazon ECS Command Line Interface (CLI).

Using Amazon ECS CLI

7

Amazon ECS **Command Line Interface** (**CLI**) is a command-line tool used to create, update, and monitor ECS clusters and tasks. Amazon ECS CLI supports the Fargate launch type. To create a container application with ECS CLI, Docker Compose (v1 or v2) is required. In this chapter, we shall use ECS CLI to launch an ECS cluster of the Fargate launch type in Windows PowerShell.

In this chapter, we will learn about the following:

- Setting up the environment
- Installing ECS CLI
- Installing AWS Tools for Windows PowerShell
- Configuring ECS CLI
- Setting up prerequisites for Fargate
- Registering the task execution policy
- Creating an ECS cluster
- Creating a security group
- Granting security group ingress
- Creating a compose file
- Configuring ECS specific parameters
- Deploying the compose file to the cluster
- Listing the running containers on the cluster
- Listing the container logs
- Scaling the tasks on the cluster
- Accessing the WordPress service
- Deleting the service and the cluster

Setting up the environment

If PowerShell is not already installed, download and install PowerShell 3.0 or a later version. Windows Management Framework 3.0 includes PowerShell 3.0:

1. Log in to PowerShell as an Administrator for which right-click on PowerShell application, and select **Run as administrator**
2. Verify that the version is 3.0 with the `get-host` command
3. Enable script execution with the following command, which allows all user-created scripts to run, and all scripts downloaded from the internet would need to be signed:

   ```
   Set-ExecutionPolicy RemoteSigned
   ```

We also need to obtain the AWS Security credentials represented with an **Access Key**, which consists of an **Access Key ID** and **Secret Access Key**:

1. To obtain the security credentials, select **My Security Credentials** from the account dropdown.
2. In the confirmation dialog, click on **Continue to Security Credentials**.
3. The **Your Security Credentials** page is displayed; select **Access keys**. Security credentials only display the **Access Key ID** and not the **Secret Access Key**. Unless the Access Key ID and the Secret Access Key were recorded earlier, create a new access key with **Create New Access Key**.
4. A **Create Access Key** dialog indicates that the access key has been created.
5. Click on the **Show Access Key** link.
6. Copy the **Access Key ID** and **Secret Access Key**. Set the environment variables `AWS_ACCESS_KEY_ID` and `AWS_SECRET_KEY`.

Installing ECS CLI

To install ECS CLI on PowerShell, first run PowerShell as an administrator by right-clicking on Windows PowerShell and selecting **Run as administrator**:

1. Subsequently, run the following command to create a new item of type directory at the specified path:

   ```
   New-Item -ItemType "directory" -Path "C:\Program
   Files\Amazon\ECSCLI"
   ```

2. Download and install ecs-cli `ecs-cli-windows-amd64-latest.exe` to application `ecs-cli.exe` in directory `C:\Program Files\Amazon\ECSCLI\`.

> **Invoke-WebRequest -OutFile 'C:\Program Files\Amazon\ECSCLI\ecs-cli.exe'**
> **https://s3.amazonaws.com/amazon-ecs-cli/ecs-cli-windows-amd64-latest.exe**

3. Add `C:\Program Files\Amazon\ECSCLI` to the `PATH` environment variable. Output the `ecs-cli` version:

> **ecs-cli --version**

The preceding commands run in PowerShell, as shown in the following screenshot:

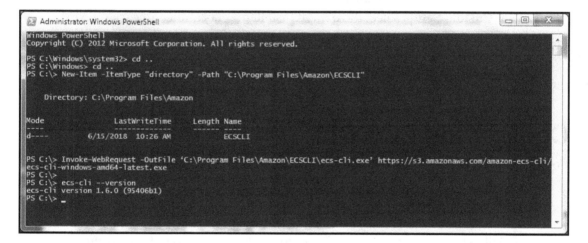

Installing AWS Tools for Windows PowerShell

Next, install AWS Tools for Windows PowerShell, which is used to manage AWS services, including ECS from PowerShell:

1. Download the MSI Installer file (`AWSToolsAndSDKForNet_sdk-3.3.231.0_ps-3.3.225.1_tk-1.14.0.1`) for AWS Tools for Windows PowerShell from `https://aws.amazon.com/powershell/`.
2. Double-click on the MSI Installer to launch the **AWS Tools for Windows Setup** wizard. Click on **Next** in the Welcome screen.
3. In **End-User License Agreement**, accept the agreement and click on **Next**.
4. In **Custom Setup**, select the default installation **Location** and click on **Next**.
5. In **Read to install AWS Tools for Windows**, click on **Install**. AWS Tools for Windows starts to get installed.
6. When the AWS Tools for Windows installation has completed, click on **Finish.**

Configuring ECS CLI

Configuring the ECS CLI involves the following two configurations:

- Configure an ECS cluster with the Fargate launch type
- Configure an ECS CLI profile

Next, we shall discuss each of these configurations. The syntax to configure a cluster is as follows:

```
ecs-cli configure --cluster cluster_name --default-launch-type launch_type
--region region_name --config-name configuration_name
```

The different command parameters in the `ecs-cli` configure command are discussed in this table:

Command parameter	Description	Value to set
`--cluster`	Name of an existing ECS cluster or a new cluster to create	`hello-world`
`--region`	AWS region	`us-east-1`
`--default-launch-type`	Launch type	`FARGATE`
`--config-name`	Configuration name	`hello-world`

1. Run the following command in PowerShell to configure an ECS cluster:

```
ecs-cli configure --cluster hello-world --region us-east-1 --default-
launch-type FARGATE --config-name hello-world
```

2. Create a directory, `C:\PowerShell`, for PowerShell and run the preceding command from the directory. As the command output indicates, the ECS CLI cluster configuration `hello-world` gets saved:

```
PS C:\PowerShell>
PS C:\PowerShell> ecs-cli configure --cluster hello-world --region
us-east-1 --default-launch-type FARGATE --config-name hello-world
time="2018-01-09T15:26:52-08:00" level=info msg="Saved ECS CLI
cluster configuration hello-world."
PS C:\PowerShell>
```

Setting up a CLI profile

The command syntax to configure an ECS CLI profile is as follows:

```
ecs-cli configure profile --profile-name profile_name --access-key
$AWS_ACCESS_KEY_ID --secret-key $AWS_SECRET_ACCESS_KEY
```

The different command parameters in the `ecs-cli` configure profile command are discussed in this table:

Command parameter	Description	Value to set
`--profile`	Name of an existing ECS cluster or a new cluster to create	`hello-world`
`--access-key`	AWS access key ID	Value would be different for different users
`--secret-key`	Secret access key	Value would be different for different users

1. Create an ECS CLI profile, `hello-world`, in which the variables need to be substituted with the `AWS Access Key ID` and `Secret Access Key`, which would be different for different users:

   ```
   ecs-cli configure profile --access-key $AWS_ACCESS_KEY_ID --
   secret-key $AWS_SECRET_ACCESS_KEY --profile-name hello-world
   ```

2. As the output from the command indicates, an ECS CLI profile gets saved:

   ```
   PS C:\PowerShell> ecs-cli configure profile --access-key Abcdef --
   secret-key D+d+KidQel/myUXJi/hJjtk --profile-name hello-world
   time="2018-01-09T15:46:15-08:00" level=info msg="Saved ECS CLI
   profile configuration hello-world."
   ```

3. As an alternative to creating a `hello-world` profile (or some other profile name), a default ECS profile may be created using the `-StoreAs` default parameter:

   ```
   PS C:\PowerShell> Set-AWSCredential -AccessKey AKIAJ4DECNW6BFYN5PNA -
   SecretKey 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 -StoreAs default
   ```

Setting up prerequisites for Fargate

In addition to configuring an ECS CLI profile, we need to set up the following prerequisites to create an ECS cluster with the FARGATE launch type:

- Create a task execution role
- Register the task execution policy
- Create the task execution role

A task execution role is required to be created for a Fargate task to be able to download a Docker image and send and save container logs in CloudWatch. Create an IAM policy, `execution-assume-role.json`, in the `C:\PowerShell\` directory, and copy and save the following JSON listing to the policy file:

```
{
   "Version": "2012-10-17",
   "Statement": [
     {
       "Sid": "",
       "Effect": "Allow",
       "Principal": {
         "Service": "ecs-tasks.amazonaws.com"
       },
       "Action": "sts:AssumeRole"
     }
   ]
}
```

Create the task execution role with the following command in PowerShell:

```
New-IAMRole -RoleName ecsExecutionRole -AssumeRolePolicyDocument (Get-Content -Raw C:\PowerShell\execution-assume-role.json)
```

As the output from the command indicates, a task execution role gets created:

```
PS C:\PowerShell> New-IAMRole -RoleName ecsExecutionRole -AssumeRolePolicyDocument (Get-Content -Raw C:\PowerShell\execution-assume-role.json)
Path    RoleName          RoleId                    CreateDate           Description
----    --------          ------                    ----------           -----------
/       ecsExecutionRole  AROAIRRZ5LMXLR6QPZQJC     1/9/2018 3:07:16 PM
```

Registering the task execution policy

Next, register the task execution policy with the following command in PowerShell:

```
Register-IAMRolePolicy -RoleName ecsExecutionRole -PolicyArn arn:aws:iam::aws:policy/service-role/AmazonECSTaskExecutionRolePolicy
```

The preceding command does not generate any output, and the task execution policy gets registered.

Creating an ECS cluster

Having configured the prerequisites, next we shall create an ECS Fargate cluster. Run the following command in PowerShell to create a cluster:

```
esc-cli up
```

As the command output indicates, a cluster gets created using the cluster configuration set up earlier. A VPC and two subnets also get created:

```
PS C:\PowerShell> ecs-cli up
←[36mINFO←[0m[0002] Created cluster ←[36mcluster←[0m=hello-world
←[36mregion←[0m=us-east-1
←[36mINFO←[0m[0003] Waiting for your cluster resources to be created...
←[36mINFO←[0m[0004] Cloudformation stack status
←[36mstackStatus←[0m=CREATE_IN_PROGRESS
←[36mINFO←[0m[0065] Cloudformation stack status
←[36mstackStatus←[0m=CREATE_IN_PROGRESS
 VPC created: vpc-6e021915
 Subnet created: subnet-2c02dd4b
 Subnet created: subnet-f2d50bdc
 Cluster creation succeeded.
 PS C:\PowerShell>
```

Access the ECS Console in a web browser and the `hello-world` cluster gets listed, as shown here:

Creating a security group

Next, create a Security group using the VPC created in the previous section on creating a cluster. The AWS region is required to be specified in the following command, if not configured in persisted/shell defaults:

```
$groupid = New-EC2SecurityGroup -VpcId "vpc-6e021915" -Region "us-east-1" -
GroupName "hello-worldPSSecurityGroup" -GroupDescription "EC2-VPC from
PowerShell"
```

List the EC2 security group with the following Get-EC2SecurityGroup command:

```
Get-EC2SecurityGroup -Region "us-east-1" -GroupId $groupid
```

The EC2 security group gets listed, as shown here:

If required, the EC2 security group may be removed with the following command:

```
Remove-EC2SecurityGroup -Region "us-east-1" $groupid
```

Granting security group Ingress

Next, add a security group rule to allow inbound access on port 80 with the Grant-EC2SecurityGroupIngress cmdlet, using the following commands run in the sequence listed:

```
$ip1 = new-object Amazon.EC2.Model.IpPermission
$ip1.IpProtocol = "tcp"
$ip1.FromPort = 80
$ip1.ToPort = 80
$ip1.IpRanges.Add("0.0.0.0/0")
```

```
Grant-EC2SecurityGroupIngress -GroupId $groupid -Region "us-east-1" -
IpPermissions @($ip1)
```

Subsequently, run the `Get-EC2SecurityGroup` cmdlet again and, as the output here
indicates, the Ingress permissions get set on the EC2 security group:

```
Administrator: Windows PowerShell                                                         _ □ X
PS C:\PowerShell> $ip1 = new-object Amazon.EC2.Model.IpPermission
PS C:\PowerShell> $ip1.IpProtocol = "tcp"
PS C:\PowerShell> $ip1.FromPort = 80
PS C:\PowerShell> $ip1.ToPort = 80
PS C:\PowerShell> $ip1.IpRanges.Add("0.0.0.0/0")
PS C:\PowerShell> Grant-EC2SecurityGroupIngress -GroupId $groupid -Region "us-east-1" -IpPermissions @($ip1)
PS C:\PowerShell> Get-EC2SecurityGroup -Region "us-east-1" -GroupId $groupid


Description        : EC2-VPC from PowerShell
GroupId            : sg-8c7dafc7
GroupName          : hello-worldPSSecurityGroup
IpPermissions      : {Amazon.EC2.Model.IpPermission}
IpPermissionsEgress : {Amazon.EC2.Model.IpPermission}
OwnerId            : 672593526685
Tags               : {}
VpcId              : vpc-6e021915


PS C:\PowerShell> _
```

We shall be creating an ECS task for WordPress only, but if a MySQL database is also to be
configured in the same task, we would also need to add an ingress rule for port `3306`,
which is exposed by the MySQL database. Run the following commands in the sequence
listed to add ingress for port `3306`:

```
$ip2 = new-object Amazon.EC2.Model.IpPermission
$ip2.IpProtocol = "tcp"
$ip2.FromPort = 3306
$ip2.ToPort = 3306
$ip2.IpRanges.Add("0.0.0.0/0")
Grant-EC2SecurityGroupIngress -GroupId $groupid -Region "us-east-1" -
IpPermissions @($ip2)
```

Subsequently, run the `Get-EC2SecurityGroup` command. As the output here shows,
ingress for port `3306` also gets added:

```
Administrator: Windows PowerShell                                    ─ □ X

PS C:\PowerShell> $ip2 = new-object Amazon.EC2.Model.IpPermission
PS C:\PowerShell> $ip2.IpProtocol = "tcp"
PS C:\PowerShell> $ip2.FromPort = 3306
PS C:\PowerShell> $ip2.ToPort = 3306
PS C:\PowerShell> $ip2.IpRanges.Add("0.0.0.0/0")
PS C:\PowerShell> Grant-EC2SecurityGroupIngress -GroupId $groupid -Region "us-east-1" -IpPermissions @($ip2)
PS C:\PowerShell> Get-EC2SecurityGroup -Region "us-east-1" -GroupId $groupid


Description        : EC2-VPC from PowerShell
GroupId            : sg-8c7dafc7
GroupName          : hello-worldPSSecurityGroup
IpPermissions      : {Amazon.EC2.Model.IpPermission, Amazon.EC2.Model.IpPermission}
IpPermissionsEgress : {Amazon.EC2.Model.IpPermission}
OwnerId            : 672593526685
Tags               : {}
VpcId              : vpc-6e021915



PS C:\PowerShell> _
```

Creating a compose file

ECS CLI supports Docker compose versions 1 and 2, and we have used version 2 for the example compose file for WordPress. Create a `docker-compose.yml` file in the `C:/PowerShell` directory, and copy the following listing to the file:

```
version: '2'
services:wordpress:
    image: wordpress
    ports:
      - "80:80"
    logging:
      driver: awslogs
      options:
        awslogs-group: hello-world
        awslogs-region: us-east-1
        awslogs-stream-prefix: wordpress
```

The Docker compose file specifies a `wordpress` service based on the `wordpress` Docker image and exposes port `80`. CloudWatch logging is configured using the `awslogs` driver, which is the only supported driver for the Fargate launch type.

Configuring ECS specific parameters

We also need to create an **ECS specific parameters** file, `ecs-params.yml`, which defines resource (CPU and memory) settings for the task to create in addition to setting the Network Mode as `awsvpc`, which is the only supported Network Mode for the Fargate launch type. The run parameters include the network configuration for subnets, security groups, and setting the `Assign public IP` option for the task to `ENABLED`. The subnets are obtained from the output of the `ecs-cli up` command. The security group is obtained from the output of the `Get-EC2SecurityGroup -Region "us-east-1" -GroupId $groupid` command, as listed earlier:

```
version: 1
task_definition:
  task_execution_role: ecsExecutionRole
  ecs_network_mode: awsvpc
  task_size:
    mem_limit: 0.5GB
    cpu_limit: 256
run_params:
  network_configuration:
    awsvpc_configuration:
      subnets:
        - "subnet-2c02dd4b"
        - "subnet-f2d50bdc"
      security_groups:
        - "sg-8c7dafc7"
      assign_public_ip: ENABLED
```

Deploying the compose file to the cluster

The `ecs-cli compose service up` command deploys a Docker compose file to a cluster. The command may optionally be parameterized with the command options discussed in this table:

Parameter	Description	Default value
`--project-name`	Project name	The current directory
`--ecs-params`	ECS params file to use	The `ecs-params.yml` in the current directory
`--create-log-groups`	Creates CloudWatch Log groups for container logs	

--file	Docker compose file	The `docker-compose.yml` file in the current directory

Run the following command in which the `--project-name` and `--create-log-groups` options are used. We don't need to use the other options, as the required files are in the current directory:

```
ecs-cli compose --project-name hello-world service up --create-log-groups
```

The Docker compose file gets deployed on the `hello-world` cluster. The output from the command is shown here:

The `hello-world` cluster lists one running task, as shown here:

Click on the `hello-world` cluster link to display its details. The service created is listed in the **Services** tab. Click on the service link as shown here to list the details:

The service **Details**, which include the name of the **Cluster** name, **Status**, **Task definition**, **Launch type**, **Platform version**, **Desired count**, **Pending count**, and **Running count** get displayed, as shown here:

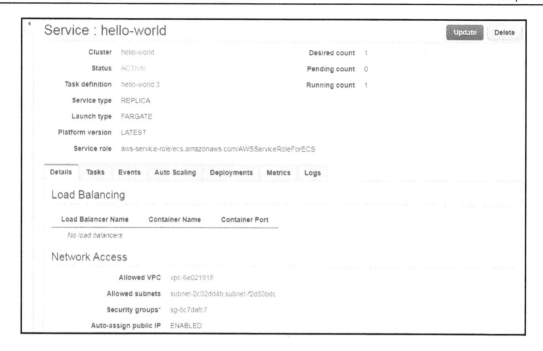

To find the task details, select the **Tasks** tab and click on the task link as shown here:

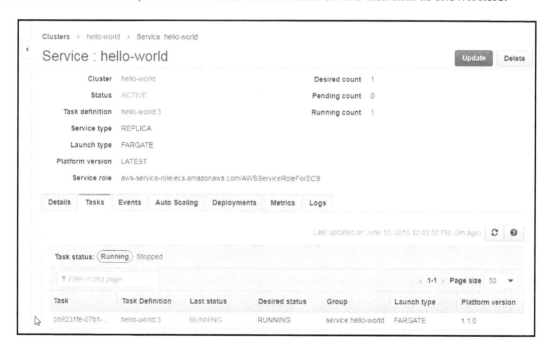

The task details get displayed, as shown in the following screenshot. The **Public IP** at which the task may be accessed is also listed:

Scroll down for the **Containers**. The wordpress container gets listed, as shown in the following screenshot:

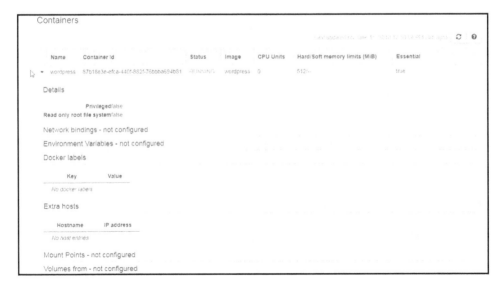

Because we configured logs, **Log Configuration** is displayed in the container details, as shown here:

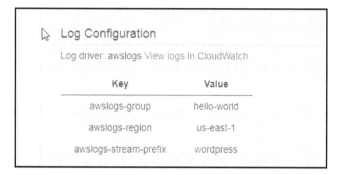

Click on the **View logs in CloudWatch** link to display the CloudWatch logs, as shown in the following screenshot:

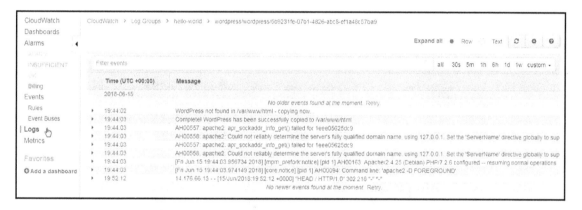

Listing the running containers on the cluster

To list the running containers on the cluster, run the following command:

```
ecs-cli compose --project-name hello-world service ps
```

The one Docker container gets listed as shown in the following screenshot. The container's State, Ports, and Task Definition also get listed:

Listing the container logs

To list the container logs, copy the task ID (the task ID is the container name `substring` before the `/`) from the container name, and run the following command:

```
ecs-cli logs --task-id 0c23d765-88c5-46cd-a317-9db243590c89 -follow
```

The container logs get displayed as shown in the following screenshot:

Scaling the tasks on the cluster

To scale the cluster to two tasks, as an example, run the following command:

```
ecs-cli compose --project-name hello-world service scale 2
```

As the output here indicates, the `desiredCount` and `runningCount` get set to 2:

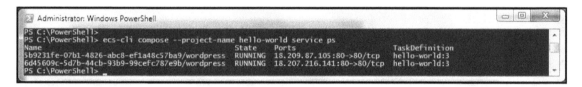

Subsequently, list the running tasks:

```
ecs-cli compose --project-name hello-world service ps
```

Two tasks get listed, as shown here:

The **Running tasks** in the `hello-world` cluster are also listed as **2**, as shown in the following screenshot. Click on the `hello-world` cluster link:

Select the **Tasks** tab and two tasks get listed, as shown in the following screenshot:

Accessing the WordPress service

To access the WordPress service, open the public IP of one of the tasks in a web browser. Select a language and click on **Continue**. The welcome page for the WordPress application gets displayed as shown in the following screenshot. Click on the **Let's go!** button:

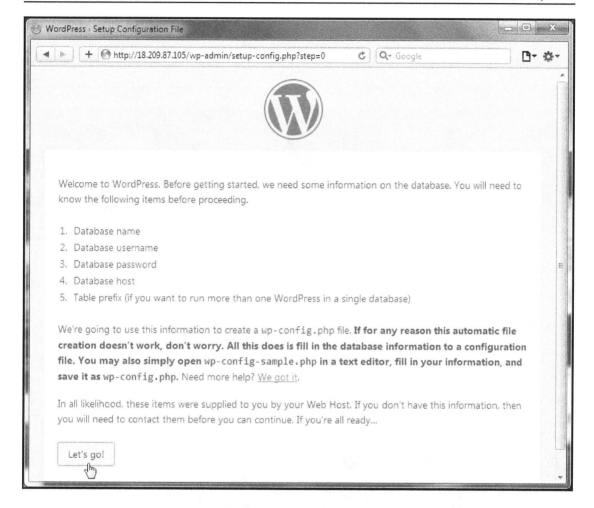

Specify the database connection details and click on **Submit** to access the WordPress dashboard. The connection details shown below may need to be modified from the default settings.

Deleting the service and the cluster

To delete the service and the associated tasks, run the following command:

```
ecs-cli compose --project-name hello-world service down
```

As the output shown here indicates, the running count and desired count for the tasks gets set to **0**, and the `hello-world` service gets deleted. The service has to be scaled down to **0** before deleting the service:

Delete the cluster with the following command:

```
ecs-cli down -force
```

Select **y** at the command prompt **Are you sure you want to delete your cluster?**. The `hello-world` cluster and all associated resources get deleted. If the cluster does not get deleted due to timeout, or due to some of the resources not getting deleted as shown in the following screenshot, run the preceding command again:

Alternatively, delete the **CloudFormation** stack associated with the cluster directly by selecting **Actions | Delete Stack** in the AWS **CloudFormation** console, as shown in the following screenshot:

In the **Delete Stack** confirmation dialog, select the stack resources not yet deleted and click on **Yes, Delete**, as shown here:

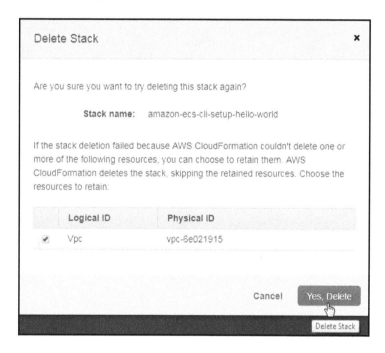

Run the `ecs-cli down -force` command again after deleting the **CloudFormation** stack directly and the cluster should get deleted, as shown here:

Summary

In this chapter, we discussed using the ECS CLI to create a cluster of the launch type Fargate. Subsequently, we deployed a Docker compose file on the cluster to run a task for the Docker `wordpress` image. We discussed listing logs and running containers, and also demonstrated scaling the service.

This chapter brings to a conclusion the Amazon Fargate Quick Start guide. Amazon Fargate is a launch type for the Amazon **Elastic Container Service** (**ECS**). At the time of writing, there is no native AWS integration between Amazon **Elastic Kubernetes Service** (**EKS**) and AWS Fargate.

Other Books You May Enjoy

If you enjoyed this book, you may be interested in these other books by Packt:

Effective DevOps with AWS
Nathaniel Felsen

ISBN: 978-1-78646-681-5

- Find out what it means to practice DevOps and what its principles are
- Build repeatable infrastructures using templates and configuration management
- Deploy multiple times a day by implementing continuous integration and continuous deployment pipelines
- Use the latest technologies, including containers and serverless computing, to scale your infrastructure
- Collect metrics and logs and implement an alerting strategy
- Make your system robust and secure

AWS Automation Cookbook
Nikit Swaraj

ISBN: 978-1-78839-492-5

- Build a sample Maven and NodeJS Application using CodeBuild
- Deploy the application in EC2/Auto Scaling and see how CodePipeline helps you integrate AWS services
- Build a highly scalable and fault tolerant CI/CD pipeline
- Achieve the CI/CD of a microservice architecture application in AWS ECS using CodePipeline, CodeBuild, ECR, and CloudFormation
- Automate the provisioning of your infrastructure using CloudFormation and Ansible
- Automate daily tasks and audit compliance using AWS Lambda
- Deploy microservices applications on Kubernetes using Jenkins Pipeline 2.0

Leave a review - let other readers know what you think

Please share your thoughts on this book with others by leaving a review on the site that you bought it from. If you purchased the book from Amazon, please leave us an honest review on this book's Amazon page. This is vital so that other potential readers can see and use your unbiased opinion to make purchasing decisions, we can understand what our customers think about our products, and our authors can see your feedback on the title that they have worked with Packt to create. It will only take a few minutes of your time, but is valuable to other potential customers, our authors, and Packt. Thank you!

Index

www.ingramcontent.com/pod-product-compliance
Lightning Source LLC
Chambersburg PA
CBHW080529060326
40690CB00022B/5074